MW01194365

LAW & ORDER
SVU: CONFIDENTIAL

Everything We Love About the Show We Can't Stop Watching

NEAL E. FISCHER

EPIC INK

CONTENTS

INTRODUCTION

DUN-DUN.

You've heard it. You've felt it. You've probably had it as a ringtone on your phone. That iconic sound isn't just a noise—it's a rallying cry for superfans of *Law & Order: Special Victims Unit*. For twenty-five years, *SVU* has viciously grabbed us by the shirt collar (as only Elliot Stabler can do) and thrown us into the world of "especially heinous" crimes and the unforgettable characters who solve them. But *SVU* isn't just a show . . . it's a cultural phenomenon, a weekly ritual, a binge-watch obsession. And if you need proof beyond a reasonable doubt that it's everyone's favorite crime obsession, look no further than *Exhibit A*: as of March 2025, there have been over 570 episodes of *SVU* (and counting!), making it `the longest-running prime-time drama in television history!` From Emmy wins to universal acclaim, social media trends to popular culture, *SVU* has transcended its procedural format and become a full-fledged institution forever secure in its place in the zeitgeist.

For fans, *SVU* is not just a show; it's a way of life. They passionately dissect plotlines, dedicate entire social media profiles to actor Christopher Meloni's glutes (arguably the "Best Butt in Prime Time"), and ship characters—especially the slowburn, will-they-won't-they dynamic of Olivia Benson and Elliot Stabler (a.k.a. "Bensler"). If you're one of many fans who constantly get that pesky "Are you *still* watching *Law & Order: Special Victims Unit*?" alert on your screen after hours of binge-watching—accept it as a badge of honor. But those of you who don't share that merit badge may wonder: Why is *SVU* so beloved? What makes it so comforting? And why are women drawn to a show that, frankly, often centers on the harsh realities of trauma and assault? Like Munch ranting about a conspiracy theory, let's take a deeper dive to find the truth . . .

COLD COMFORT

At its heart, *SVU* thrives on its themes of justice and empathy. In our world, justice can often feel elusive or nonexistent, and *SVU* offers a cathartic escape. Week after week, Benson and her team fight tirelessly for victims and survivors while showing compassion and resilience at every turn. And for fans of the show in marginalized communities, particularly people of color, the show's portrayal of law enforcement as fair, dependable, unprejudiced, and unwaveringly committed to justice for *everyone* is a form of wish fulfillment. It's a vision of the world where the system works, where victims are heard, where the police are fair, and where criminals face consequences. Critics may call the show a fantasy, but true fans understand that it represents how the justice system should be and not the imperfect reality in which we live. But why are especially heinous crimes comforting to watch? The answer lies in the show's formula.

Every episode of *SVU* follows a safe and reliable pattern:

- **Crime**
- **Investigation**
- **Resolution**

This structure offers emotional safety and guarantees that, however dark the episode gets, justice will prevail by the end credits. Having a world where good triumphs over evil, even fictionally, brings comfort.

HOW PEOPLE WATCH *SVU*

For many, watching *SVU* isn't just a weekly appointment—it's the perfect background companion that pairs well with just about anything. Whether you're tuning in with full focus or letting it play while tackling life's little tasks, here are just a few ways people find themselves caught in the grip of the show:

- While folding laundry (as interrogation room suspects air out their own dirty laundry).
- Running on a treadmill (to ensure you're always faster than the show's creeps).
- Working from home (nothing beats the steady hum of crime-fighting white noise).
- Relaxing in a hotel room (because, let's face it, it's always on a hotel room TV).
- During a sick day on the couch (the only cure? Benson delivering swift justice).
- On a long flight (because turbulence pales in comparison to the suspense of *SVU*).

For most viewers, especially women, the show's soothing predictability is also its superpower. Do fans love to joke about the fact that an episode's first suspect rarely did it, while a celebrity guest most surely did? Yes. And do fans understand that if an extra disclaimer is put at the top of the episode, stating that the story is fictional and does not depict any real person or event, then it's definitely based on a real person or event? Of course! But that's why it's so enjoyable. It's a slice of calorie-free dessert before bedtime—pure, cozy bliss, with a side of crime.

It may seem odd that women want to repeatedly watch other women go through pain, trauma, and vicious crimes. Yet *SVU* validates women's experiences and portrays survivors with dignity and empathy, largely because of the show's feminist hero, Olivia Benson. She listens, she believes, and she fights for justice. In a world where survivors rarely come forward due to fear of shame or retribution, the show offers a different story—a place where survivors are supported, encouraged, and vindicated. Sure, these fictional victims get justice within just a few days (and not years of litigation like in reality), but how else are they supposed to wrap up a story in sixty minutes?

The appeal of *SVU* goes beyond entertainment. Studies have shown that viewers of SVU are more likely to understand consent, recognize abusive behavior, and feel empowered to take action. In many ways, it's an educational tool disguised as a crime drama. Perhaps the reason it resonates with women so much is because it centers on their stories, their complexities of survival, and the power required for them to heal. From Benson leading the precinct to Assistant District Attorney (ADA) Cabot fighting for convictions, Rollins going undercover, and Dr. Warner saving the day, the show is unabashedly female and empowering. And what's cooler than seeing a mother balance childcare and her career while getting shot at, kidnapped, and still kicking ass? The show even inspired star Mariska Hargitay herself. In 2024, Hargitay shared her own painful journey as a survivor of sexual assault, stating, "A man raped me in my thirties. It wasn't sexual at all. It was dominance and control." For years, she pushed the trauma away, but the show gave her the courage to confront it. She credits her advocacy work and portrayal of Olivia Benson as integral to her healing. "I have, so many times, encountered people that have said because of this show, they knew what to do after an assault," she said, adding, "Most of all, they didn't feel alone anymore. To me, when I started hearing those stories, that's when I knew it wasn't a TV show anymore. It was so much more." Hargitay's role on the show has become synonymous with strength. She's a symbol whose unwavering dedication to victims across New York City has inspired real-life careers in law enforcement, social work, and advocacy.

THE OTHER SIDE OF THE AISLE

But no discussion of *SVU* would be complete without hearing from the opposing counsel: the critics. Some argue the show engages in "Copaganda," idealizing law enforcement while glossing over systemic issues like police misconduct and bias. It often portrays perpetrators as middle-to-upper-class white offenders, sidestepping the reality of racial disparities in policing. One can also point to the portrayal of swift justice (taking just days instead of months or years) as misleading to viewers unfamiliar with the criminal justice system where plea deals are much more common. Some episodes have been called out for oversimplifying complex issues or presenting overly optimistic views of how survivors are treated. And even Olivia Benson isn't immune to criticism. Fans have noted instances of her pressuring victims to testify, making promises of protection she can't always keep, and in later seasons, bending the rules for herself while reprimanding her team for doing the same. One of the show's stars, Diane Neal (ADA Casey Novak), once admitted such concerns in an X thread (formerly Twitter): "I'm embarrassed to admit, I used to think the way it worked on the show was like real life. Then I found out the hard way I was wrong." Given these arguments, and the fact that the show has aired during the age of #MeToo and public calls to reexamine policing in America, it's remarkable that *SVU* still resonates so deeply across audiences—an appeal that proves it transcends genre, politics, and ideologies. Fans might be anti-police, but they're pro-Olivia Benson. While those in law enforcement or legal positions may critique its "realism," most fans and critics share this mantra: **"It's not perfect, but it's ours."**

To underscore the show's monumental legacy, in March 2024, Rockefeller Center hosted an extravagant pop-up event that turned New York City into a playground for fans to celebrate twenty-five years of *SVU*. It included:

- **Drinks named after characters, like Benson's Captain-ccino, Carisi's Classic Americano, Fin's Iced Tea, and Cup of Joe Velasco.**

- **Friendship bracelets saying *Dun Dun, WWOBD* (What Would Olivia Benson Do?), and *Elite Squad*—25 percent of proceeds went to Hargitay's Joyful Heart Foundation.**

- **Appearances by cast members like Ryan Buggle (Noah Porter-Benson), Kevin Kane (Det. Terry Bruno) and Octavio Pisano (Det. Joe Velasco).**

- **Fifty thousand limited edition MTA cards for commuters.**

This party, attended by thousands of superfans, wasn't just an acknowledgment of the show's longevity but a celebration of its cultural significance. The anniversary was only strengthened in September 2024 when the Smithsonian's National Museum of American History accepted one of Olivia Benson's classic costumes into their collection. As a cultural phenomenon, *SVU* has sparked political and social debates, inspired advocacy, and provided comfort to millions on a daily basis. Its success lies not just in its longevity but in its ability to adapt, remain relevant, and rip stories from the headlines. It's more than entertainment—it's a shared experience and a beacon of hope in an imperfect world.

With over 25 seasons and over 570 episodes, there is no way every character, memorable line, guest star, plot point, and detail could fit into these pages, but they're a good place to start. `For SVU isn't merely a TV show—it's a way of life.` And if anyone disagrees with you, throw the book at them. Literally. Throw *this* book at them and call your favorite ADA, who will have them charged, indicted, tried, convicted, and jailed faster than you say "Khashisti."

THE CREATION

THESE ARE THEIR STORIES

Before *SVU* became a record-breaking cultural phenomenon, it began as the relentless vision of Dick Wolf—the wizard of the procedural crime drama. Wolf wasn't satisfied with the status quo of television and saw a new franchise that would push boundaries; explore the darker, more psychologically complex aspects of crime; and highlight the interesting and often messy lives of those sworn to protect us. In 1990, viewers were exposed to a chilling narration before every episode of *Law & Order* that ended with four words that would define the franchise for decades: "These are their stories." Those four words would become synonymous with riveting drama, thrilling plotlines, and twist endings.

To tell the story of how *SVU* came to exist, we must go back to the man behind it all . . .

It's hard to imagine a time before *Law & Order: SVU* graced the airwaves. In fact, it's hard to remember a time before any Dick Wolf shows were on TV. In 2024, there were eleven Dick Wolf produced programs all running at full speed:

Chicago Fire
Chicago P.D.
Chicago Med
Cold Justice
FBI
FBI: Most Wanted
FBI: International
Law & Order: Special Victims Unit
Law & Order: Organized Crime
Law & Order Toronto: Criminal Intent
Law & Order (the original show!)

THE MAKING OF A MASTERMIND

Born and raised in New York City, Dick Wolf started as a successful advertising copywriter, tasked with coining slogans for major brands. One Wolf original is for Crest toothpaste: "You can't beat Crest for fighting cavities." But despite his *Mad Men*–esque journey through thirty- and sixty-second ads, Wolf's true passion was elsewhere. **"I decided I didn't want to sell toothpaste for the rest of my life,"** he later said.

He was writing screenplays on the side, hoping to break into Hollywood. Wolf's persistence paid off when he sold his first script, *Skateboard* (1978), cowritten with George Gage. As he gained recognition as a screenwriter, Wolf pivoted to television in the mid-1980s, landing a gig as a staff writer on *Hill Street Blues*. It was here that he received his first-ever Emmy nomination for Outstanding Writing in a Drama Series for his work on "What Are Friends For?" (S6, E9; 1985). It was just a taste of all the accolades to come. The show also introduced him to his friend and future collaborator, composer Mike Post.

Wolf then became a producer and writer on *Miami Vice*, where he developed his **signature Dick Wolf style—sharp, focused storytelling that cut to the core of human conflict.** Subsequent shows (*Gideon Oliver, Christine Cromwell, Nasty Boys,* and *H.E.L.P.*) were each canceled after one season on the air, but he continued to have success in film writing. And as the decade came to a close, Wolf took everything he had learned from advertising, film, and television and channeled the highs and lows into one groundbreaking idea—a crime show that wouldn't just last a season, but would change television history forever.

NIGHT & DAY

After his time on *Miami Vice* and his own short-lived series, Wolf wanted to create a fresh approach to the increasingly stale crime genre. He came up with a new series called *Night & Day*—but wisely (at least for fans) changed the name to *Law & Order*. The concept was a series that depicted an optimistic picture of America's criminal justice system.

KEY FEATURES:

1. **The first half would follow two homicide detectives (a senior and a junior detective) with their commanding officer investigating a violent crime.**
2. **The second half would follow the district attorney's office and the following trial.**
3. **These stories wouldn't just be creations from the stellar writer's room, but would be based on real cases making the headlines—the birth of his "ripped from the headlines" signature storytelling.**

When Wolf pitched it to Universal, they noticed that it was similar to a very short-lived series called *Arrest and Trial* that followed a police officer arresting a suspect in the first half and the defense attorney proving their innocence in the second half. But it was too formulaic. Wolf wanted the detectives to be fallible and for the stories to be realistic in all aspects of police work and prosecution—to make a calling card not only for himself but for the genre as a whole. One of his first moves was departing from only the defense attorneys being heroes so he could highlight the prosecution and give these brave men and women their own "day in court" on television.

THE BEST DEFENSE

It's the prosecution who puts the bad guys away, but defense attorneys have long made great dramatic characters in film, TV, and literature. Here are twelve standouts, because, as a good defense attorney, you need to convince twelve people of your client's innocence:

- Annalise Keating (*How to Get Away with Murder*)
- Atticus Finch (*To Kill a Mockingbird*)
- Ben Matlock (*Matlock*)
- Elle Woods (*Legally Blonde*)
- Jake Brigance (*A Time to Kill*)
- Jennifer Walters a.k.a. She-Hulk (*She-Hulk: Attorney at Law*)
- Matt Murdock a.k.a. Daredevil (*Daredevil*)
- Mickey Haller (*The Lincoln Lawyer*)
- Perry Mason (*Perry Mason*)
- Phoenix Wright (*Ace Attorney*)
- Saul Goodman (*Breaking Bad; Better Call Saul*)
- Vincent Gambini (*My Cousin Vinny*)

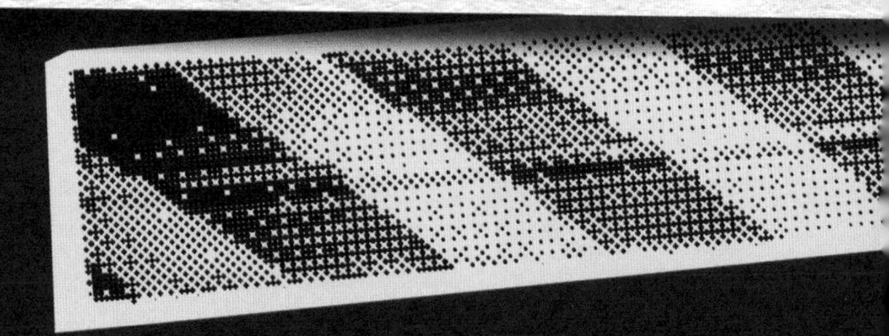

THE MOTHERSHIP

The original *Law & Order* is known to passionate devotees of the expansive Dick Wolf universe as "The Mothership" due to its impact on television. The series launched several successful spin-offs and actors' careers and served as the foundation for all that came after it. But its journey to the small screen was anything but easy. Though initially pitched to multiple networks, *Law & Order* had numerous setbacks. Fox showed interest early on but ultimately passed. CBS commissioned a pilot episode and even reserved a slot for their 1990–91 fall programming season. However, CBS thought the show was too intense for audiences and decided not to air it. They also saw it as too much of an ensemble cast with no "star quality" and thought it lacked any real "breakthrough" actors. Instead of taking a chance on the show, they renewed another season of their own crime drama *Jake and the Fatman*, which lasted five seasons for the network.

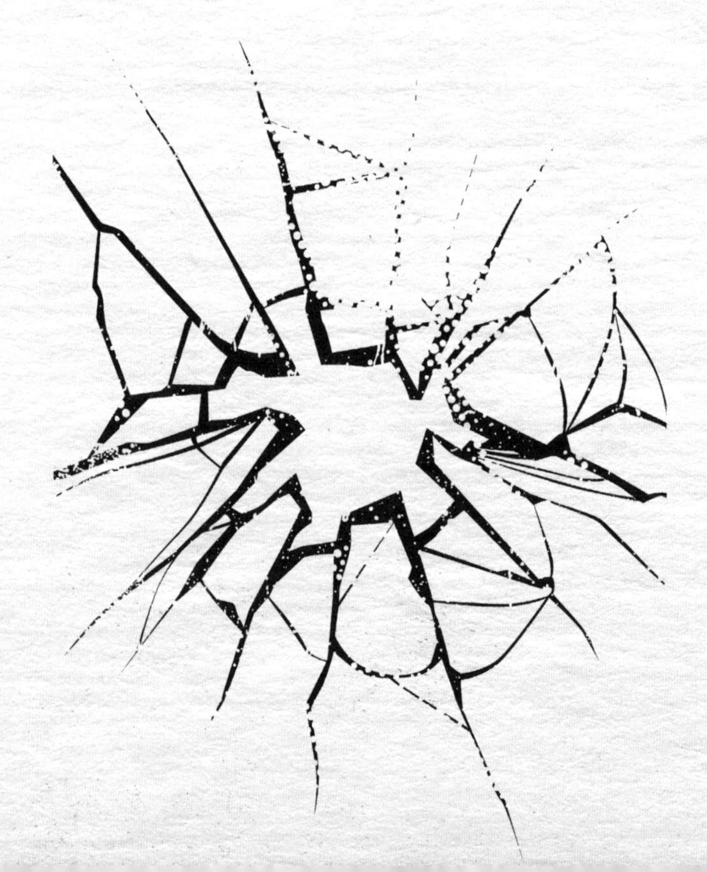

THE ORIGINAL CAST OF LAW & ORDER:

District Attorney (DA) Adam Schiff:

The stoic and pragmatic head of the DA's office

Played by Steven Hill

Executive ADA Ben Stone:

Prosecutor torn between legal obligations and moral imperatives

Played by Michael Moriarty

ADA Paul Robinette:

Dedicated to justice and navigating complex racial issues

Played by Richard Brooks

Detective Max Greevey:

Seasoned detective with experience and gravitas

Played by George Dzundza

Detective Mike Logan:

Brash and street-smart detective whose passion for justice gets him into trouble

Played by Chris Noth

Captain Donald Cragen:

Tough and loyal veteran who transfers to the Special Victims Unit in the show's first spin-off

Played by Dann Florek

A LITTLE HELP FROM MY FRIENDS

Universal Television (who had bankrolled the pilot) still believed in Wolf's new concept and encouraged him to pitch it to NBC, who would eventually pick up the show . . . but not without hesitation. Many NBC executives were skeptical, feeling *Law & Order* was too gritty and too unconventional for audiences. However, it had two key supporters: Brandon Tartikoff and Warren Littlefield. In a 1997 *Los Angeles Times* piece, written shortly before his death, Tartikoff admitted that he only bought *Law & Order* because he wanted another Dick Wolf show, *Nasty Boys* (a series about ninja cops in Las Vegas), and they were a package deal.

A PRIME TIME RÉSUMÉ

TV executive Brandon Tartikoff was the head of the entertainment division of NBC from 1981 to 1991 and was inducted into the Television Hall of Fame in 2004. He is credited with turning around NBC's reputation in the '80s with several hit TV series, including but not limited to:

- *Hill Street Blues*
- *L.A. Law*
- *ALF*
- *Family Ties*
- *The Cosby Show*
- *Cheers*
- *Seinfeld*
- *The Golden Girls*
- *Miami Vice*
- *The A-Team*
- *Punky Brewster**

* Tartikoff helped develop this sitcom and named the title character after a girl he had a crush on in school. Tartikoff tracked down the real Punky (Peyton B. Rutledge), got legal permission to use the name Punky, and she made a cameo as a teacher in Season 2, Episode 9, "The Search."

The original *Law & Order* pilot episode ("Everybody's Favorite Bagman") would become Episode 6 of the first season, while a new episode, "Prescription for Death," served as the show's true premiere on September 13, 1990. After a rocky start, critics and audiences were on board. Adding to its popularity was the use of real New York City locations (instead of backlots in Hollywood), which gave it an authenticity rarely seen on network television and put New York's unique energy, diversity, and rawness on full display.

The filmmaking style was also notable. Pairing handheld cameras and stark lighting for the first half of episodes (during the investigation) and more polished lighting and camera work for the second half in the courtroom (for the trials) created visual storytelling that redefined the genre. *TV Guide*, in its first article about the show, even remarked on the gritty palette of this new show by noting that despite it being in color, **"you'd swear that it was shot in grainy black and white."**

In 1992, two years after it premiered, the show received its first Emmy nomination for Outstanding Drama Series, and for a decade, it would be nominated every year for this prestigious award—ultimately taking it home once, in 1997. By the mid-'90s, *Law & Order* was a staple in households across America. It presented ethical dilemmas based on real-life crimes ("ripped from the headlines") and tasked middle America with deciding whether justice was achieved by the end of each week's episode—a signature of the series.

RIPPED FROM THE HEADLINES

Dick Wolf and his team often referred to *The New York Post* (and its sensational stories that captivated the public) as a sort of bible for episode inspiration. Some of the Season 1 episodes that kicked off this trend:

"Indifference" — Inspired by the Lisa Launders case, this episode included a rare spoken and visual disclaimer pointing out the actual real-life conclusion to the case, marking it as the only episode in the franchise to do so.

"The Serpent's Tooth" — This episode drew inspiration from the infamous Menendez brothers' case, portraying two brothers accused of murdering their wealthy parents.

"The Violence of Summer" — Partially inspired by the 1989 Central Park Jogger case, this episode features Samuel L. Jackson and marks the screen debut of the late Philip Seymour Hoffman.

"Life Choice" — A compilation of several cases, this is Dick Wolf's favorite first-season episode, whose controversy cost NBC $800,000 in sponsor pullouts and meant it was not included in reruns until 2001. It was key to attracting the show's serious fanbase, and in 2009, *TV Guide* ranked it No. 62 in its list of television's 100 Greatest Episodes.

Law & Order had proven itself to be a sleeper hit, and the decision to focus on storytelling over star power became a defining feature of the series. The interchangeable cast and self-contained episodes resulted in seamless transitions when actors departed. The series would be made famous by beloved characters like Detective Lennie Briscoe (Jerry Orbach), Executive ADA Jack McCoy (Sam Waterston), Lieutenant Anita Van Buren (S. Epatha Merkerson), Detective Ed Green (Jesse L. Martin), and Detective Rey Curtis (Benjamin Bratt).

As the years went on, *Law & Order* built a strong following, but Dick Wolf had another idea brewing . . . one that would once again redefine the genre.

THE BIRTH OF *SVU*

Despite the growing success of *Law & Order*, Wolf wanted to go darker and delve into the psychology of both perpetrators and victims, especially in sexual offenses. One real-life case stuck with him: the 1986 "Preppy Murder" of Jennifer Levin by Robert Chambers, where a "rough sex" defense strategy fascinated and disturbed him. He explored the case in *Law & Order*'s "Kiss the Girls and Make Them Die" (S1, E4; 1990), but Wolf wanted to go deeper.

Thus, *Law & Order: Sex Crimes* was born. It was a concept that left no ambiguity about its focus. It was all in the title. It would take the most taboo crimes and sensitive topics—sexual assault, child abuse, and domestic violence—and put them front and center on network television. But NBC found the title too provocative, fearing it might alienate viewers. Wolf compromised and the show became *Law & Order: Special Victims Unit*—named after a real division within the NYPD—but even with a name change, it wouldn't be smooth sailing to convince the network that this was their next big hit.

Behind the scenes, executives were cautious. They wondered if audiences could handle such dark material on a weekly basis. Typical primetime programming was about family squabbles, lessons of the week, comedy, drama—not sex crimes and violence against vulnerable populations. And the advertisers were nervous, too. This was NBC, after all, not HBO. Could a primetime network show handle crimes like sexual assault and domestic violence without exploitation? And what would set this apart from The Mothership and other procedurals? Executive producer Ted Kotcheff, a veteran film director, had an answer: *SVU* would be cinematic, noir-like, and emotionally charged—less about courtroom resolutions and more about the victims and detectives. Like The Mothership, it would have the dependable detective beats, suspect beats, and courtroom drama, but it would take it a step further and a step darker in its storytelling, all without veering into sensationalism—a delicate balance that would become *SVU*'s hallmark. The creative team stressed that the show wasn't about shock value. It wasn't about scaring viewers into calling the network. It was about telling stories that mattered, that were often ignored or dismissed, for the first time. Thankfully, NBC understood.

CASTING *SVU*

After it received its much-deserved green light, the stakes were high for *SVU*. The show simply wouldn't work unless it had a great cast. And thanks to its subject matter, more eyes were on the show than normal. `The series needed actors who would be slam dunks.`

After weeks of deliberation, searches, auditions, and debates, the last auditions were to be held in the iconic Rockefeller Center. This final round wasn't limited to a casting director, a camera, and a few people in a room—NBC and USA Network executives were along for the ride too.

It all came down to finding the perfect Benson and Stabler.

THE FINALISTS

Detective Olivia Benson:

- Samantha Mathis
- Reiko Aylesworth
- Mariska Hargitay

Detective Elliot Stabler:

- Tim Matheson
- Nick Chinlund
- Christopher Meloni

But there was an instant winning combination. Even before they auditioned, Meloni and Hargitay immediately clicked—so much so that they kept producers waiting while they finished sharing a joke. Hargitay remembers that they were getting along so well that when it came time to pair actors up for a chemistry test, she thought, "I want to be with that guy!"

So, you can call it luck, you can call it fate, but either way, it was clear that *SVU* had found its perfect pair. The heart of the show.

BUILDING THE SQUAD

Now that the show had its stars, it was time to surround them with an ensemble formed from old faces, deliberate choices, and a few serendipitous circumstances.

> **Dann Florek** would reprise his role of Captain Don Cragen from *Law & Order*'s first three seasons to bring established gravitas, authority, and continuity.

> **Richard Belzer** carried over his already established character, Detective John Munch, from *Homicide: Life on the Street.* He joked that the deal occurred because "Dick Wolf and Tom Fontana [showrunner of *Homicide*] got drunk at a party."

> **Michelle Hurd** was cast as Detective Monique Jeffries after having worked with Dick Wolf three times before, as a day player on *Law & Order* and the short-lived *Players*, and as a recurring cast member (ADA Reynolds) on *New York Undercover.*

> **Dean Winters** got the role of Detective Brian Cassidy thanks to Richard Belzer, who recommended him to Dick Wolf after their work together on *Homicide: Life on the Street.*

THE WONDERFUL WORLD OF

OZ

Did you know over two hundred actors and actresses have appeared on both *SVU* and HBO's *Oz*? Below is a list of *SVU* favorites, who, before suiting up for the Sixteenth Precinct, spent a little time at Oswald State Correctional Facility as inmates, undercover cops, and a prison chaplain:

- **Christopher Meloni**
- **BD Wong**
- **J.K. Simmons**
- **Dean Winters**
- **Robert John Burke**
- **Terry Serpico**
- **Mike Doyle**
- **Lance Reddick**

CREATING THE VISUAL WORLD OF *SVU*

From day one, *SVU* needed to look and feel different from *Law & Order*. Executive producer Ted Kotcheff was determined to make *SVU* stand apart, saying, "Out of ego, I wanted my show to be different. I didn't want to be a step-child [of *Law & Order*]. These are difficult emotions, dealing with children and people who are such a puzzle."

Law & Order had a raw, shaky, documentary-style look, but *SVU* would add a smoother and more immersive visual feel similar to big-screen movies. In lieu of mostly handheld cameras, *SVU* would introduce significantly more polished motion techniques such as:

> **Dolly Shots** – A classic Hollywood technique used since the earliest days of filmmaking, the dolly shot creates smooth, polished, and graceful movement. Imagine a tiny train track laid down on set, with a camera mounted on a wheeled cart (the dolly) that glides forward, backward, side-to-side, or even in circles. Unlike handheld shots, dolly shots add a professional quality that draws viewers into the scene. If there's a slow camera push-in on someone's face, that's most likely a dolly. The famous dramatic zoom in on Chief Brody's face in *Jaws* (called a dolly-zoom or the *Vertigo* effect in honor of director Alfred Hitchcock) was achieved using a camera on a dolly and a zoom lens working in tandem to create the effect. The magic of a dolly shot is controlled precision. The camera moves just as planned.

> **Steadicam Shots** – This technique, made immensely popular amongst film crews after its use in *Halloween* (1978) by legendary cinematographer Dean Cundey (*Jurassic Park, Back to the Future, Apollo 13*), allows for long, fluid, controlled camera movements without shakes, and most notably, without tracks. It's widely used in television because scenes can be shot quickly without complex camera or lighting setups—just mount the camera on the Steadicam, essentially a floating arm that's attached to a vest worn by the camera operator, and your expert operator can move almost anywhere. Some famous examples? The camera gliding behind Danny's tricycle in *The Shining*, the iconic tracking (moving) shot through the Copacabana in *Goodfellas*, or pretty much every frame and scene in *1917*, which follows soldiers in what is designed to look like one continuous shot.

The easiest way to understand *SVU*'s style is just to watch the first ten minutes of any early episode. Instead of choppy, rapid cuts, the camera glides around the actors in the bullpen as detectives discuss cases, creating a real-time feel. These shots usually start after Cragen appears and says something to the effect of, "Okay team, what do we have?" As the camera glides through a scene, detectives move to multiple positions to deliver their lines, anticipating each other's moves to create a natural rhythm, ping-ponging dialogue back and forth and creating the authenticity of a real squad room.

But if you really want to pin down how the series' look has changed from season to season, look no further than the subtle shifts in lighting styles and shooting formats. Seasons 1 through 12 were shot with film cameras, giving the show a high-contrast, shadowy, and moody lighting style. Since Season 13, the show has used digital cameras and adopted a flatter, evenly lit, almost sterile look surely designed to save time and money.

HOMEWORK: Watch an episode of *SVU* from Season 2 and from Season 20 back-to-back and see if you can notice the differences!

THE PRODUCTION DESIGN

In the beginning, *SVU* had to set itself apart from The Mothership while retaining the same quality as the original. That starts with the sets, props, and set dressings. *SVU* sets aren't just backdrops—they're lived-in spaces meticulously designed, from the over-used pencils on cluttered desks, real NYPD posters, and coffee-stained paper down to the handwritten notes and worn filing cabinets most likely purchased during the Gerald Ford administration. Before the show entered its teen seasons, the main bullpen, where much of the action takes place amid detectives' desks, phones, break areas, etc., looked and felt gritty and worn. You can smell the cork on the picture boards. The stale coffee. The mounds and mounds of late paperwork. It's a level of verisimilitude that is rarely seen on network television—especially when you add the extensive on-location shoots in New York City, which became an integral part of the show's success. Then, as the show began to evolve and modernize, the clutter turned into clean lines, the construction looked more high-end, and the lights went from flickering to bright LEDs.

Helping production design immensely was the real-world design of New York City itself. From sprawling Central Park to the shadowy alleyways in Brooklyn and busy streets of Midtown, the city is the perfect backdrop for the unit's cases. Due to lack of space and affordable real estate in Manhattan, *SVU* first filmed in North Bergen, New Jersey while its writing team primarily worked from Los Angeles. Still, Kotcheff and crew managed to captured New York's dual nature—its glittering beauty and its dark and gritty corners. What better place to be than a city that reflects the complexity of the crimes the Special Victims Unit explores.

IMMEDIATE RECEPTION AND GROWING POPULARITY

SVU premiered on September 20, 1999, and early reviews praised its bold risk-taking and the chemistry of its leads. While it carried the *Law & Order* brand, *SVU* proudly set itself apart. *The New York Times* praised its "crackling-sharp" storytelling and gave it a strong endorsement that pushed it outside the shadow of its predecessor by saying, "Any fear that this franchising would result in a pallid McLaw-and-Order burger vanish with tonight's premiere." *Entertainment Weekly* acknowledged that while *SVU* divided longtime fans of The Mothership—some felt it was too similar, others not enough—the show's dense storytelling made it a compelling addition. The show was recognized by several outlets as clearly having the potential for longevity. Over twenty-five years later, it looks like the critics were right.

Though it never topped the Nielsen ratings, *SVU* built a dedicated fanbase that grew through word of mouth and syndication marathons on the USA Network, turning it into a binge-worthy phenomenon. By Season 4, the show had solidified itself as a primetime powerhouse, pulling in millions of loyal viewers each week. That same season, *SVU* reached a turning point: Hargitay earned her first Emmy nomination for Outstanding Lead Actress in a Drama Series and the show became a go-to spot for guest stars, with early career performances from Abigail Breslin and Hayden Panettiere, who delivered pulse-pounding portrayals that proved that *SVU* had the right stuff. Right out of the gate, *SVU* was destined to become a popular show, but the cultural phenomenon it grew into (with worldwide acclaim) couldn't have been predicted by anyone.

THE EVOLUTION OF *SVU*

You don't have to be Taylor Swift to put things you love into eras! A show that's been around this long is bound to have distinct periods, each with its own stories, cast, and tone. Ask any fan, filmmaker, or Reddit user, and you'll get a slightly different take on how *SVU* has evolved. But for most, the show is generally categorized like this:

1. **The Benson and Stabler Years (Seasons 1–12):** The foundation of *SVU*'s success, driven by Olivia Benson and Elliot Stabler. Their chemistry anchored the show and was built around their contrasting approaches to crimefighting—empathy vs. intensity.

2. **The Post-Stabler Years (Seasons 13–21):** With Stabler's exit, Benson took center stage. This era explored her trauma, resilience, and leadership, while new cast members brought fresh dynamics. If 1.0 was a two-hander, 2.0 was an ensemble show with Benson at the helm.

3. **The Return of Stabler (Seasons 22–Present):** Christopher Meloni's return (and the emergence of his new spin-off *Law & Order: Organized Crime*) rekindled the magic of the early years. Stabler's presence added new tension and emotional stakes as he and Benson navigated their past and present while staying relevant.

A FAMOUS FAN

Speaking of eras, Taylor Swift famously named her cat Olivia Benson after Mariska Hargitay's beloved character. In a playful nod to their real-life friendship, Hargitay later adopted a cat and, in a reference to one of Swift's songs, named it Karma.

THE BREAKDOWN

THE RECIPE

For over two decades, the show has `perfected the art of procedural drama, balancing structure with fresh storytelling` that keeps audiences hooked. While *SVU* may seem formulaic, it's anything but. Like a Hallmark Christmas movie or classic action flick, it paints within familiar lines, but adds unexpected twists, deeply emotional cases, and character-driven narratives that elevate it from cookie cutter to cinematic couture.

Ironically, *SVU*'s formula is really its lack of a rigid formula. While some episodes deliver clear verdicts, others leave things unresolved, encouraging viewers to reflect on what they've seen. The show isn't just about solving crimes—it examines ethical dilemmas, the justice system's flaws, and the people who police it. At its core, it has a consistent and reliable framework:

1. **Discovery of the crime**
2. **Investigation**
3. **Legal proceedings**
4. **Resolution**

Think of this process as the foundation of a house. Every episode will have it, and every episode needs it. Then, the writers build off that foundation by ingeniously subverting expectations through strategic story disruptions. Procedurals often get a bad rap, with viewers calling them lazy, tired, or predictable; but *good* procedurals take that foundation and build something truly unique each and every week.

Early on, the *SVU* team realized they didn't have to copy the same structure as The Mothership or other procedurals. Not to burst your spoiler bubble, but most cop shows introduce their villain early on in Act 1 or Act 2 of the episode (mostly so audiences will recognize them forty minutes later at the climax). However, *SVU* took that staple and twisted it around. Here, villains could be introduced in the teaser, halfway through an episode, or even in the final scene. Instead of maintaining one overarching tone for all episodes in a season, the writers could shift from psychological thriller to action film to meditative character study, sometimes in the same episode. They might even sideline main characters for an entire episode. One of *SVU*'s writers, Robert Nathan, put it best when describing the difference in formula between The Mothership and *SVU* by saying, "One's a sonnet, the other's free verse."

Another reason for the show's longevity? Its ability to stay *of the moment*. While some argue that later seasons lean too much on "ripped from the headlines" cases (and become heavy-handed melodrama), the show's real strength is its commitment to exploring social issues from new angles. Does it always stick the landing? Definitely not. But wouldn't you rather watch a show that takes risks and doesn't just repeat itself? The show still clearly follows one of its writers' only, original rules: Don't be ordinary, and don't be lazy.

THE WRITING OF *SVU*

Writing for a police procedural requires both artistry and precision. The format has been around for seventy-five years with shows like *Dragnet* (1951–59), *Hill Street Blues* (1981–87), and *NYPD Blue* (1993–2005) taking charge. But how do you stand out?

In its early years, *SVU* ditched the traditional writer's room. Instead, writers worked independently of each other, which gave each episode a unique tone and voice, acting more like mini-movies rather than singular episodes in a larger, serialized arc. To help strengthen the show when it came to legal, law enforcement, and scientific terms, **SVU writers had an open dialogue with legal and forensic experts**, with some of the writing staff being former law enforcement professionals. This lent the show accuracy—well, TV accuracy. In real life, DNA results don't come back in thirty seconds. If only they could.

The show also broke new ground by bringing more female writers into the fold, ensuring authentic perspectives. But it wasn't all sunshine and roses amongst *SVU*'s talented scribes: with new opportunities came high expectations. Writer and producer Dawn DeNoon recalled that many writers were let go if their scripts weren't up to the standards the filmmakers demanded. For better or worse, this constant turnover and fear of being fired created a pressure-cooker environment that helped fuel the visceral, edge-of-your-seat storytelling among not just the writers, but everyone behind the camera.

ACT STRUCTURE: THE HEINOUS STORY ACTS OF *SVU*

To truly understand *SVU*'s writing, look at its structure. Early seasons followed a four-act structure with a teaser; newer seasons contain a five-act structure with a teaser. Want to track it at home? `Watch the commercials—they often signal the act breaks` which come after a cliffhanger, captivating one-liner, gut-punch reveal, or actor emoting their butt off as the camera slowly zooms in on their face.

1. **Teaser/Cold Open — The Hook:** Often the discovery of a dead body. Over time, *SVU* shifted from dead bodies to survivors, creating a stronger emotional connection with the viewer. The whole point of this teaser is to pull viewers in and not let them go.

2. **Act 1 — The Setup:** Detectives begin investigating—making calls, collecting evidence, and gathering leads. Exposition is laid out. The conflict, stakes, and key players are introduced.

3. **Act 2 — The Investigation Gets Messy:** The case takes unexpected turns. Detectives face unreliable witnesses, dead ends, and red herrings. A suspect might emerge but prove too slippery to charge. New evidence raises more questions.

4. **Act 3 — Escalation & Breakthrough:** The investigation hits a boiling point. A shocking revelation, confession, or unexpected twist changes everything. Here a witness flips, a crucial forensic detail cracks the case, or the detectives finally begin connecting the dots—just in time for a dramatic confrontation.

5. **Act 4 — Climax & Showdown:** The perpetrator is usually confronted, arrested, or charged. Legal proceedings begin, offering plea deals, trials, or moral dilemmas. The episode's core theme—justice, power, or institutional failure—comes into focus.

6. **Act 5 — The Aftermath:** Closure (or lack thereof). Some episodes end with justice served, others with lingering questions or processing from the main characters. It might tie up loose ends, set up future storylines, or drop one last twist to leave viewers shaken.

WHAT IS A COLD OPEN?

A technique dating back to the late 1950s, a cold open is a short, attention-grabbing scene before the opening credits, designed to hook viewers. Whether dramatic, suspenseful, surprising, or comedic, it skips a traditional introduction and dives right in without warning—hence, the "cold" in cold open.

Like many procedurals, *SVU* uses cold opens to create immediate tension or, occasionally, to inject a bit of dark humor. Some notable examples include:

- "BABES" (S10, E6; 2008)
  A lighthearted restaurant scene (and an order of flambé) turns into a burning body in the street.

- "LOOPHOLE" (S8, E13; 2007)
  WWE's Bill Goldberg plays a PCP-fueled suspect who rampages through the precinct and throws Stabler through a window before Fin knocks him out with a chair.

- "RIDICULE" (S3, E10; 2001)
  Benson and Stabler discover an autoerotic asphyxiation gone wrong, ending with a darkly comedic quip from Stabler.

SHOWRUNNERS: THE ARCHITECTS OF *SVU*

Every great TV series has a heartbeat, and for *SVU*, that heartbeat is its showrunners. These creative visionaries shape not just the plotlines, but the very tone and identity of the series.

While Dick Wolf is the ultimate creator (like a police commissioner) and executive producers like Ted Kotcheff (Seasons 1–13) and Julie Martin (Seasons 14–26) ensure quality (like Internal Affairs), a showrunner is like Captain Cragen: the day-to-day general in the trenches overseeing everything from writers, casting, budgeting, props, editing, and hiring directors. It's one of the most coveted yet demanding jobs in television, requiring time, energy, and creativity. It's not for the faint of heart—no major decision happens without the showrunner's approval.

The *SVU* showrunners:

- **Robert Palm:** Season 1
- **David J. Burke:** Season 2
- **Neal Baer:** Seasons 3–12
- **Warren Leight:** Seasons 13–17, 21–23
- **Rick Eid:** Season 18
- **Michael S. Chernuchin:** Seasons 19–20
- **David Graziano:** Seasons 24–26
- **Michele Fazekas:** Season 27–Present (the program's first female showrunner!)

THE SVU MANTRAS

Creator Dick Wolf has two mantras displayed on leather signs in his office: "It CAN be done" and "It's the writing, stupid." These phrases not only highlight the high standards demanded by Wolf and company but also reflect the impactful storytelling that's defined *SVU* in each and every episode.

NEAL BAER: THE GOLDEN ERA OF *SVU*

Neal Baer's tenure cannot be understated. For many fans, his run is quintessential *SVU*. A Harvard-trained doctor and seasoned TV writer (*ER*), Baer joined Season 2 at Dick Wolf's request, bringing medical accuracy and emotional depth to the show. At the time, *SVU* was in flux—Season 1 showrunner Robert Palm had left due to the dark subject matter and his replacement, David J. Burke, struggled to connect with the team. Baer took over midway through Season 2, proving his worth by rewriting "Pixies" (S2, E9; 2001) in a single weekend.

His impact extended beyond his writing. He deftly helmed complicated productions, often overseeing fourteen episodes at once. He elevated Dr. Melinda Warner (Tamara Tunie) from background medical examiner (ME) to key team member by integrating her medical expertise (which was *his* expertise) and added scientific rigor just as *CSI: Crime Scene Investigation* made forensics mainstream. He also developed Dr. George Huang (BD Wong), whose psychological profiling helped audiences understand *why* criminals acted the way they did. But Baer's true legacy lies in his focus on societal issues—such as the HIV crisis, untested rape kits, and, years before they came into the public eye, transgender rights.

Under his direction, *SVU* prioritized victims and their trauma over detectives' personal lives, a balance that shifted after his departure.

WARREN LEIGHT: THE EVOLUTION OF EMOTION

If Baer defined *SVU*'s golden era, Warren Leight ushered in its emotional renaissance. A Tony Award-winning playwright, Leight brought character-driven storytelling to *SVU*, emphasizing personal struggles alongside procedural drama. He introduced pivotal characters like Detective Amanda Rollins (Kelli Giddish) and Detective Nick Amaro (Danny Pino), whose battles with addiction, family turmoil, and marital strife added emotional resonance. Most notably, Benson evolved from detective to squad leader to adoptive mother, making her the show's emotional core—and turning the show into *LIV & Order*, for better or worse.

Leight and Mariska Hargitay (as producer) championed trauma-informed storytelling, consulting experts on PTSD, abuse, and systemic corruption. Episodes no longer ended with a verdict; they explored the aftermath, portraying justice as complex rather than black and white. Leight also wove timely issues into the show, like online harassment, police accountability, immigration, and even the effects of CTE (chronic traumatic encephalopathy) on football players, keeping *SVU* fresh without losing its identity. If Baer set the foundation, Leight enriched it—ensuring the series remained relevant.

NOTABLE WRITERS

Below are some of *SVU*'s most prolific writers and their key contributions.

JULIE MARTIN (2011-PRESENT): A driving force alongside Warren Leight, known for emotional depth and high-stakes drama in episodes like “Surrender Benson,” “Dreams Deferred,” and “Heartfelt Passages.”

DAWN DENOON (1999-2011): Crafted some of the show's most unforgettable twist-filled episodes including “Raw,” “Pure,” and “Identity” (with Lisa Marie Petersen).

AMANDA GREEN (2002-2010): A former law enforcement officer who balanced procedural precision with raw emotion in “Dolls,” “Paternity,” and “Haunted.”

PATRICK HARBINSON (2002-2007): An ex-soldier turned writer who brought heart and tension to “Silence,” “911,” and “Fat”—and created fan-favorite Sister Peg!

MICHELE FAZEKAS AND TARA BUTTERS (2002-2006): Dynamic duo responsible for some of *SVU's* most gripping and controversial episodes such as “Fault,” “Loss,” and “Charisma.”

DAVID GRAZIANO (2022-2025): A recent showrunner responsible for *SVU*'s new direction, who worked alongside cowriter Julie Martin on episodes “Cornered,” “King of the Moon,” and “Blood Out.”

THE MUSIC

Most true crime junkies would agree that the *Law & Order* theme song is the gold standard of police procedurals, an auditory lightning rod that makes viewers silence all cell phones, dim the lights, and slap on an imaginary badge.

Famed composer Mike Post (arguably the greatest TV theme composer ever) was tasked by Dick Wolf to create a new theme for the original *Law & Order*. Wolf's instructions? It must be gritty, evoking the feeling of steam coming out of the streets and representing the majesty of the scales of justice. `It shouldn't just sound like New York—it should` *`define`* `it.` Post's response was a surprisingly minimalistic yet unforgettable mix of:

- **guitar**
- **electric piano**
- **a jazzy clarinet—a nod to George Gershwin's "Rhapsody in Blue."**

Post has since composed music for every *Law & Order* theme song and episode (except for *Organized Crime*), relying on minimal music during the action so that the compelling characters and intense stories reign supreme. To reiterate, Post has created a *different* theme song for each *Law & Order* series: all unique in their own right but sharing DNA with the original.

RAP SHEET

ICONIC TV THEME SONGS OF MIKE POST:

The Rockford Files (1974)

Magnum P.I. (1980)

Hill Street Blues (1981)

The Greatest American Hero (1981)

The A-Team (1983)

L.A. Law (1986)

Quantum Leap (1989)

Doogie Howser, M.D. (1989)

Blossom (1990)

NYPD Blue (1993)*

*For this theme song, Mike Post was inspired by the drum solo from "In the Air Tonight," the smash-hit, debut solo single by Phil Collins.

To some, it's known as "clank-clank"; to others, it's "chung-chung" or "doink-doink"; and to most, it's simply "Dun-Dun." Known as "The Clang" to Post, this iconic amalgamation of sounds and samples (or previously recorded audio) almost never existed. After finishing the original *Law & Order* theme, Wolf called up Post in a bind—he needed a transition sound for new title cards featuring timestamps and locations. Initially, Post refused. He was a composer, not a sound designer. But after some coaxing, he hit the studio, experimenting for two days until he landed on an unlikely, but now famous, mix of audio elements:

- **a jail door slamming shut**
- **a man striking an anvil with a hammer**
- **various drums**
- **most notably, the sound of one hundred Japanese men stomping on a wooden floor.**

You'll never listen to it the same way again, right?

When he handed in "The Clang," Post unknowingly created the signature sound of *Law & Order*—and became the composer of the most iconic audio onomatopoeia ever made. Post also jokingly calls his creation "Ching-Ching" because, `as a musical composition (and not merely a sound effect), it earns him royalties every time it plays.` Wolf teases Post that he won't be remembered for all the memorable music he wrote—just the one composition he didn't even want to do. Two notes that aren't really notes at all. And he's probably right.

LAW & ORDER: SPECIAL BINGO UNIT

With over twenty-five years of twists, turns, and tropes, you'd really need twenty-five *different* bingo cards to encompass the sheer power of the Special Victims Unit Universe or *SVUniverse*. But this one comes pretty close! If only the card had endless squares, we could have included things like:

- **Stabler smirking, or being asked if he has children.**
- **Benson calling Noah her "sweet boy," or whispering through her lines.**
- **Rollins questioning Warner.**
- **Novak using a favor to get a judge in her favor.**
- **Or Kim Rollins literally making us want to turn the TV off!**

But for now, we've included as many prompts as we could that make the game accessible for any era, season, or episode.

So, grab your card, cue up an episode, and let the games—and justice—begin.

LAW & ORDER: SPECIAL BINGO UNIT

"Call a bus!"	Suspect flees during discovery or questioning	Location: Central Park / Hospital / Alley	Miranda Rights	Detective loses temper and manhandles suspect in the box or in the field
Reprimanded in the Captain's office	The prosecution requests remand or says a defendant is a flight risk	Crime during cold open ends up being unrelated to the episode	ADA needs more evidence: "Not enough to hold/charge them"	Interviewee multitasks while being questioned
Snappy comeback or one-liner	Record is clean—not even a parking ticket	Free Space Executive Producer Dick Wolf	Rape Kit	Perp lineup in person or on a picture card: "Take your time"
Body discovered by unsuspecting citizen (dog, jogger, homeless person, etc.)	Gathering around the big evidence board or computer screen	Judge: "I'll allow it"	Suspect saying the sex was consensual; or they had sex but didn't kill the victim	Celebrity (before or during fame) is the villain
Mention of DNA or the fact that "it doesn't lie"	Blunt force trauma to the head	"One PP" /"TARU"	ME calls detectives after finding surprising but helpful intel from the body	Story is clearly "ripped from the headlines"

THE LINEUP

THE STARS

When *Law & Order: Special Victims Unit* first debuted in 1999, it introduced six compelling characters who would become TV icons. Without them, the show wouldn't be the juggernaut it is today. As the series grew, fan favorites like Detective Fin Tutuola (Ice-T), Detective Amanda Rollins (Kelli Giddish), and ADA Rafael Barba (Raúl Esparza) joined the ranks, bringing fresh perspectives and, more importantly, new energy to the Sixteenth Precinct.

One of *SVU*'s most impressive feats is finding a way to seamlessly introduce new faces while maintaining the same great storytelling, never alienating its fans. While purists may favor the OG Stabler-Benson dynamic with its will-they–won't-they energy, each of the show's twenty-six seasons has given us unforgettable characters who make us laugh, cry, and root for them as they protect and serve those who need it most. In this chapter, we'll celebrate some of the most essential and beloved characters in *SVU* history. From those who've been around the longest to recurring characters who left a lasting impact, these are the people who have shaped the show's legacy, episode after episode, season after season. And for that, we thank them.

THE VOICE OF LAW & ORDER

If you guessed that Mariska Hargitay holds the record for most appearances in *Law & Order* history, you'd be *dead* wrong. DUN-DUN. That honor belongs to Steve Zirnkilton. You might not recognize his name, but you definitely know his voice. Zirnkilton's iconic narration has set the tone for every *Law & Order* series from The Mothership to *Law & Order Toronto: Criminal Intent*! Without him, the show simply wouldn't be the same.

So how did a former politician and real estate broker from Maine land the most coveted voiceover gig in history? Ambition and perfect timing. Zirnkilton met Dick Wolf while helping him buy a house. When the sale was done, Wolf asked, "How much do I owe you?" Instead of sending a bill, Zirnkilton handed him his voiceover demo reel. The bold move paid off. Wolf hired him for promos for the short-lived series *Nasty Boys* and then asked him to narrate the *Law & Order* pilot. The rest, as they say, is history. Over the years, Zirnkilton's commanding voice has popped up on *Family Guy*, *The Rugrats Movie*, *Murderville*, and Wolf's true crime series *Blood & Money*.

This is his story.

CAPTAIN OLIVIA BENSON

PORTRAYED BY: Mariska Hargitay

FIRST APPEARANCE: "Payback" (S1, E1; 1999)

For a quarter of a century, Benson has been the soul of *SVU*, inspiring millions, redefining heroism, and becoming the longest-running live-action character in primetime history. She's been stalked, stabbed, shot, kidnapped, poisoned, tortured, and nearly blown up. Yet she still fights. As long as there are victims to avenge and barriers to break . . . Olivia Benson will be there.

Born from tragedy as the child of her alcoholic and abusive mother's rape, Benson transformed her pain into purpose. From the moment she and Stabler investigated a castrated cabbie in 1999, it was clear their dynamic would become the show's emotional core—and it remains one of the most analyzed partnerships in crime TV history. But Benson is more than one half of a pair, and she isn't just a symbol of resilience; she's a person with flaws, quirks, and sharp instincts. As the queen of the no-nonsense clapback, few things are as satisfying as watching Benson coolly dismantle a predator in the interrogation room with a cutting remark, or put an ADA in their place when they care more about winning than the victims. Even after getting poisoned with mushrooms, she still managed to continue interrogating, although it gave fans one of the most quoted lines in *SVU* history (about the captain and a pickle; you know the one), that Hargitay often jokes is when the show jumped the shark. Benson is the master of the eyebrow raise, the knowing smirk, the intense whisper, and the ultimate unimpressed stare that lets criminals know they've already lost before the conversation begins.

Beyond her fierce professionalism and dedication to the job, Benson's personal life has been anything but steady. After Stabler left in Season 12, Benson's story went into overdrive, chronicling her rise from detective to captain, mentoring detectives like Rollins, taking a cue from Cragen on how to be an effective leader, deepening her bond with Fin, and fulfilling her dream of becoming a mother when she adopted Noah. Balancing the job with raising a child was no small feat, but she embraced it with the same tenacity she brings to the SVU. She's also survived harrowing ordeals and had to deal with their resultant trauma, which has slowly hardened her into a more guarded, but no less determined, leader. This character evolution has extended to her wardrobe, as her growing authority, gravity, and strength translate to deliberately badass sharply tailored pantsuits, structured blazers, and sleek coats that exude confidence and command.

But why is Olivia Benson so iconic? Why is she, as the kids say, *Mother*? Because the line between actor and character is so blurred they've become one. "I felt like God put me on this show for a reason," Hargitay said. It's clear she doesn't just play Olivia; she *is* Olivia. Horrified by statistics she learned while researching for the role (one in three women and one in six men are survivors of sexual assault; every sixty-eight seconds in the US, someone is sexually assaulted; four to five children die every day from abuse and neglect), Hargitay founded the Joyful Heart Foundation to make a difference. Survivors began writing to her—not fan mail, but their stories. They knew she would listen and never judge. It's a testament to her portrayal: That's the power of Olivia Benson. That's the power of Mariska Hargitay.

In the real world, Mariska Hargitay proves that heroics aren't just for fictional detectives on TV screens. Here's how she's changing the world.

- CERTIFIED HERO: To better understand her character, Hargitay became a certified rape crisis counselor.

- THE JOYFUL HEART FOUNDATION: Founded by Hargitay in 2004 to support survivors of sexual assault, domestic violence, and child abuse, the foundation's End the Backlog initiative has processed thousands of untested rape kits, and its Heal the Healers program provides grants and support for the professionals who work directly with survivors of abuse and violence.

- CAPITOL HILL CRUSADER: In 2017, Hargitay testified alongside Wayne County prosecutor Kym Worthy about the discovery of 11,341 untested rape kits in Detroit. Over several years, Hargitay and Worthy collaborated to eliminate the backlog, which was officially cleared in 2022. It led to 2,616 DNA matches, 840 serial rapists identified, and 229 convictions.

- REAL-LIFE RESCUE: In 2023, Hargitay paused filming on *SVU* to help a lost little girl (who thought Hargitay was a real police officer) find her mother.

- AWARD-WINNING ADVOCATE: Hargitay coproduced the Emmy-winning documentary *I Am Evidence*, exposing the criminal justice system's failures in addressing the rape kit backlog.

Perhaps Olivia Benson is just portraying Mariska Hargitay.

DETECTIVE ELLIOT STABLER

PORTRAYED BY: Christopher Meloni

FIRST APPEARANCE: “Payback” (S1, E1; 1999)

Whether you love him, hate him, or have a crush on him, Elliot Stabler is one of the most complex characters in the *Law & Order* universe. He's a man deeply driven by justice, yet often at war with himself—a flawed, tragic hero defined by loyalty, love, and an unyielding fight to achieve balance between good and evil, even when the world refuses to align with him. Stabler grew up in Queens in a chaotic home. His father, an abusive cop, beat into him a rigid sense of right and wrong, while his mother's undiagnosed bipolar disorder created constant emotional turmoil in the household. These early experiences left him with a simmering anger that often got him in trouble. He joined the Marines young, served in Desert Storm, and earned a degree at Queens College—all while marrying his high school sweetheart and becoming a father. In other words, he was just a kid when he joined the NYPD.

On the beat, Stabler is a force of nature, and not at all "stable." His intense emotional investment makes him a good investigator, but also a liability. The interrogation room is his sparring ring, and if his sleeves are rolled up and you see the Marine tattoo—boy are you in trouble. Talk back, insult him, or *lie*, and your face meets the metal cage on the window. And since he has the badge, everything is kosher (if Cragen isn't watching). Is it right? Absolutely not. Is it captivating? Absolutely.

What truly sets Stabler apart is his unwavering loyalty to his partner, Olivia Benson. Their relationship was the heart and soul of the show's early years—a perfect balance of opposites that tempered and grounded each other. But it was the tender moments that showed us who Stabler really was: a tough but deeply caring man who wanted the best for everyone around him. He isn't perfect. His Catholic upbringing became a source of both strength and guilt that shaped his choices and struggles, but he always tries to be the best father and husband, even as his work consumes him.

After a shooting that left a teenage girl dead, Stabler abruptly retired in Season 12 without saying goodbye to Benson—a decision that left both characters (and fans) reeling. Years later, the prodigal son returned a changed man, hardened by his wife's murder and plagued by grief that reignited his relentless drive and forced him to confront his past, and perhaps his unresolved feelings for Benson. Stabler is one of those rare characters who feels larger than life yet completely real. Add Christopher Meloni's powerhouse performance, and damn—that's good TV. *SVU* might be Benson's show, but when Stabler is around, it'll always have more heart.

EXHIBIT: 8HGUE8

THE STABLER FAMILY

You can't talk about Elliot Stabler without mentioning his family. Their lives show the delicate balance between a high-stakes career and personal relationships. Here are the highlights:

KATHY STABLER (ISABEL GILLIES)
Married at seventeen, Kathy was Elliot's high school sweetheart and often acted as the glue holding their family together under the strain of Elliot's job. Initially wary of Elliot's "work wife," she and Benson grew close. After separations and reconciliation, Kathy's life tragically ended in a car bombing, devastating Elliot and driving him to seek justice.

MAUREEN STABLER (ERIN BRODERICK - TEEN AND AUTUMN MIRASSOU - ADULT)
The eldest Stabler child, Maureen often clashed with Elliot's overprotectiveness. Despite his grip, Maureen forged her own independence, attended Hudson University, and later stepped into a maternal role after Kathy's death.

KATHLEEN STABLER (HOLIDAY SEGAL - CHILD AND ALLISON SIKO - ADULT)
Marked by legal troubles (credit card fraud, DUIs), and a bipolar diagnosis, Kathleen's turbulent journey changed after treatment. She became an advocate for abuse victims and a key support system for her siblings.

DICKIE AND ELIZABETH (JEFFREY SCAPERROTTA - CHILD/ADULT, PATRICIA COOK - CHILD AND KAITLYN DAVIDSON - ADULT)

The twins had different paths. Dickie's rebellious teenage years strained his relationship with Elliot. He lost his best friend to murder, wanted to join the Army, and frequently tested Elliot's patience while still seeking his approval. Elizabeth had a quieter presence but faced challenges, including being targeted by a predator, which showcased Elliot's fierce protectiveness.

ELLIOT "ELI" STABLER, JR. (NICKY TORCHIA)

Born during Elliot and Kathy's reconciliation (and delivered with help from Benson after a car crash), Eli spiraled into substance abuse after Kathy's death before healing through therapy and family support.

BERNADETTE STABLER (HEATHER KLOBUKOWSKI - YOUNG ADULT AND ELLEN BURSTYN - ADULT)

Elliot's mother struggles with bipolar disorder, which often defined their rocky relationship. In "Swing" (S10, E3; 2008), during a manic episode, she nearly killed Elliot in a car accident. Burstyn won an Emmy for her performance.

SERGEANT ODAFIN "FIN" TUTUOLA

PORTRAYED BY: Ice-T

FIRST APPEARANCE: "Wrong Is Right" (S2, E1; 2000)

FACT: He's the knot in your stomach, he named his gun Teresa after his ex-wife, and he's the second-longest-running character in *SVU* history. And as the squad learned quickly, he just knows stuff.

Joining *SVU* in Season 2, Fin was only supposed to last four episodes, but thanks to Ice-T's larger-than-life persona, he made Fin feel real, grounded, and undeniably authentic. And thankfully he hasn't left. Originally a narcotics detective haunted by the memory of a partner who took a bullet for him, Fin evolved far beyond his street smarts. Pairing him with John Munch was a stroke of genius, creating one of TV's best cop duos. Their bond grew from initial friction to genuine friendship and was highlighted by sharp political debates and mutual respect. When Munch retired, Fin naturally transitioned into a mentor role for the SVU. Even Fin's wardrobe reflects his evolution—from pinstriped suits and a ponytail to bomber jackets, fresh sneakers, and darker colors (perhaps in tribute to his former partner).

Work is Fin's life. No excuses—just results. And he always goes the extra mile for victims and families, like when he took a bullet from a scared kid and turned it into a life lesson instead of an arrest. Above all, Fin's best trait is his loyalty. He always supports his fellow detectives and loves tracking down leads. He even has a rope guy—who also handles tides, paints, and solvents. But his relationship with Benson is the show's gift that keeps on giving. Fin is the only person Benson listens to, and the only person she admits is right. Mirroring this dynamic, Ice-T has said he'll only leave the show when Hargitay does.

The irony of Ice-T—rap pioneer, heavy metal frontman, TV icon, and the man behind "Cop Killer"—playing one of TV's most famous cops isn't lost on anyone. But Ice-T silenced skeptics long ago, and Fin's legacy is unmatched.

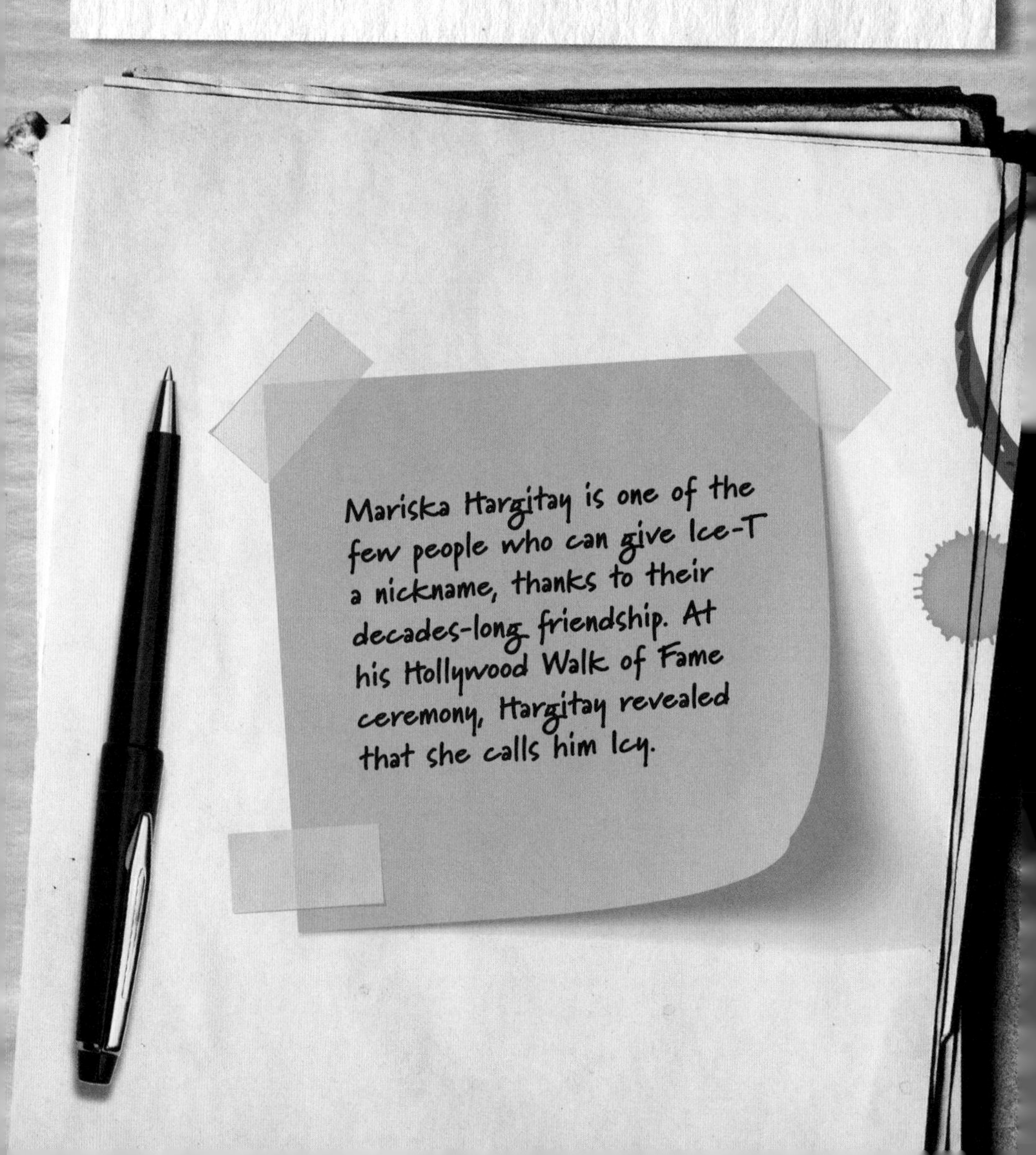

EXHIBIT: AJ

CAPTAIN DONALD CRAGEN

PORTRAYED BY: Dann Florek

FIRST APPEARANCE: “Payback” (S1, E1; 1999)

LAST APPEARANCE: “The Five Hundredth Episode” (S23, E6; 2021)

Captain Donald Cragen isn't just a name in the *Law & Order* universe; he's the show's moral compass, heart, and backbone. First introduced in The Mothership pilot as the no-nonsense captain of the Twenty-seventh Precinct's homicide unit, Cragen quickly became a fan favorite, and for fifteen seasons on *SVU*, commanded the Manhattan Special Victims Unit with strength and empathy.

Cragen's quiet resilience was shaped by his own struggles with alcoholism, which hit rock bottom after he pulled a gun on a cab driver in a drunken rage. His recovery gave him a depth few TV captains possess. But his door—and his heart—were always open. The squad was, in effect, his family. His dynamic with Benson and Stabler produced some of the show's best moments, especially when they ignored his orders, prompting him to deliver his best "in my office" dad energy.

But Cragen's greatest asset was his stress radar. He always kept a close eye on his team, fully aware of the horrors they faced each day. If they needed time off, he sent them home. And in a film noir touch that matched his vibe, early on, he kept a bottle of alcohol in his desk—not to drink, but as a nod to his past struggles. His wardrobe—shirt, tie, suspenders, and a steady look of concern—echoed his no-frills, quiet dependability. Yet small personal touches, like a jug of Red Vines on his desk or a New York Mets cap, reminded us of the man behind the badge. Whether he was complaining about 1PP, IAB, or bureaucratic red tape—or in one episode, waking up next to a dead sex worker—Cragen always captivated.

Spanning over two decades and more than four hundred appearances across the *L&O* universe, Cragen mentored detectives and navigated scandals in a career almost as long as Benson and Fin's. His legacy will always be his tough-but-fair leadership style. And while we may not know if—or when—he'll return, it's nice to imagine him enjoying some well-earned peace . . . and maybe a lunch date with Kimba.

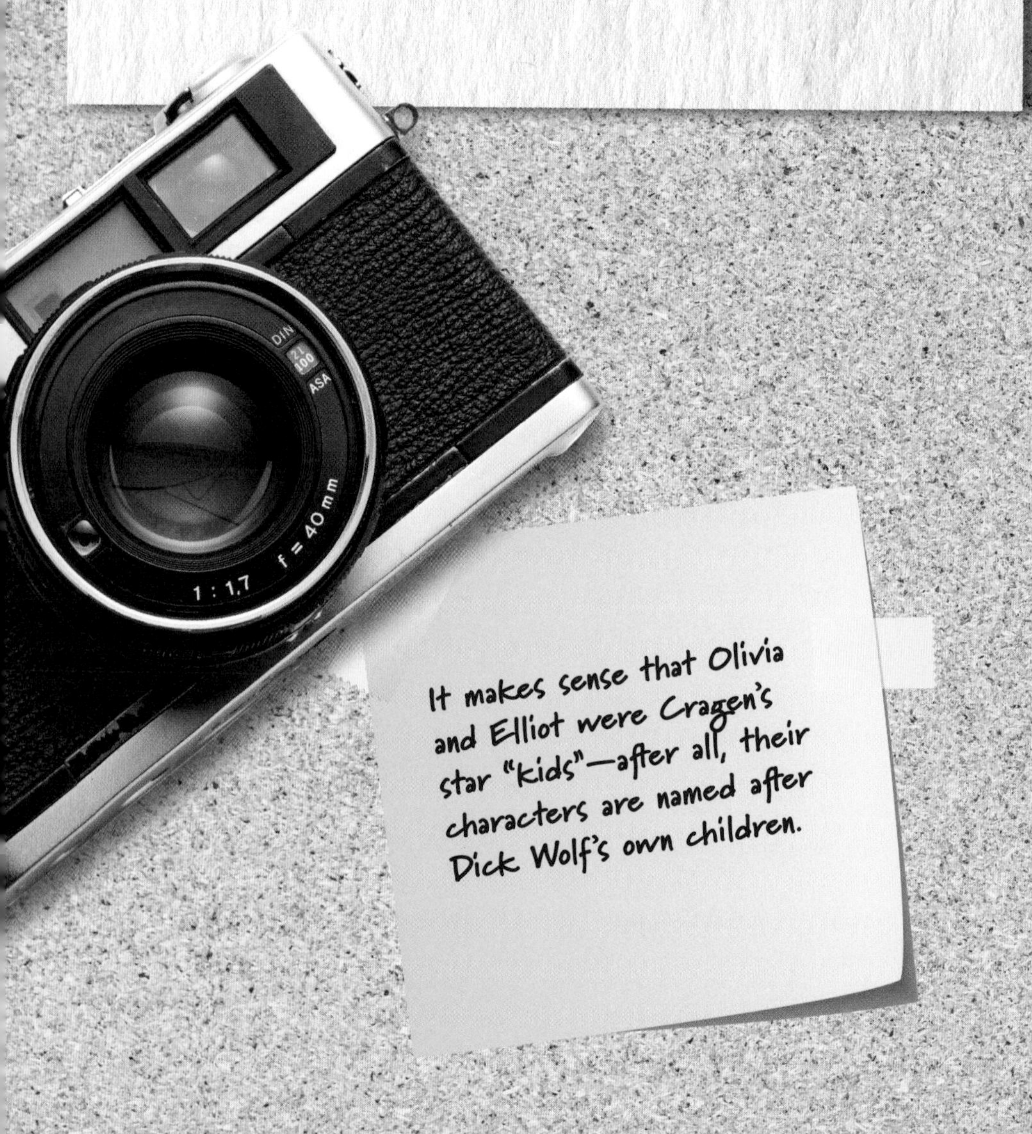

It makes sense that Olivia and Elliot were Cragen's star "kids"—after all, their characters are named after Dick Wolf's own children.

EXHIBITS: C9 / E41 / D32
404

SERGEANT JOHN MUNCH

PORTRAYED BY: Richard Belzer

FIRST APPEARANCE: "Payback" (S1, E1; 1999)

LAST APPEARANCE: "Fashionable Crimes" (S17, E20; 2016)

With sardonic wit, endless conspiracy theories, and the driest of humor, John Munch remains one of television's most iconic detectives. Munch first appeared in *Homicide: Life on the Street* and during a crossover event with The Mothership, Belzer's memorable performance impressed Dick Wolf, who invited him to join his new series—not as a new character, but as Munch. From there Munch became the ultimate TV crossover king, appearing in nearly a dozen shows including *The X-Files*, *The Wire*, *Arrested Development*, *30 Rock*, and even *Sesame Street*. His long career is a testament to Belzer's enduring performance and Munch's ability to fit into any universe—or more accurately, the Munchaverse.

On *SVU*, Munch built strong partnerships with Brian Cassidy, Monique Jeffries, and most memorably, Fin Tutuola. Munch and Fin became almost as iconic a duo as Benson and Stabler, their scenes filled with Munch's jokes balanced by Fin's eyerolls and deadpan comebacks. Beneath the sarcasm, Munch was deeply loyal to his friends. His signature look—black suits, tinted glasses, and that ever-present cynical smile—perfectly mirrored his dark yet oddly endearing worldview.

Haunted by childhood abuse and his father's suicide, Munch masked his pain with humor but never wavered in his moral compass. If a scene needed comedic relief, in walked Munch—including one fan-favorite moment where a court stenographer asked him to spell "hysterical paroxysm" in front of the court. In a touching scene after announcing his retirement, Munch babysat Benson's son, Noah, and joked to Benson that he'd already taught Noah the importance of questioning authority. According to Fin, Munch eventually moved back to Baltimore, met a divorced female rabbi, and bought back his old cop bar. While he never had any Munchkins of his own, there's no doubt they'd have shared his unique brand of cynicism and grown up to be fully functioning anti-dogmatic atheists.

Behind the character was Richard Belzer, a stand-up comedian turned actor whose razor-sharp wit and intelligence perfectly colored Munch. Like his character, Belzer was fascinated by conspiracy theories, even authoring books on everything from Princess Diana and UFOs to Elvis and JFK. Whether or not fans agreed with his theories, Belzer's charm made them listen. Belzer passed away in 2023, but thanks to streaming, Munch will always be just be a click away.

EVIDENCE
CASE NO:G0987789
Exhibit: A / B / C / D
↓
Exhibit: 170827WH

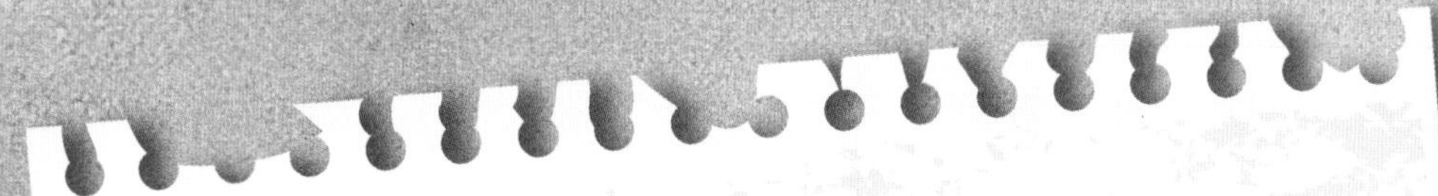

DR. GEORGE HUANG

PORTRAYED BY: BD Wong

FIRST APPEARANCE: “Pique” (S2, E20; 2001)

LAST APPEARANCE: “Depravity Standard” (S17, E9; 2015)

Portrayed with subtle grace by BD Wong, Dr. George Huang made his *SVU* debut as an FBI agent on loan. In truth, his character was only supposed to appear in four episodes (as a trial run, like Ice-T)—but after seeing him interact with the cast, Huang soon became a pillar of stability for the Sixteenth Precinct, thanks to his expert psychological profiling and collaboration skills. Huang's obsession with human behavior and how the mind works brought a unique edge to *SVU*... His more clinical, measured approach often clashed with impulsive colleagues like Stabler, but Huang always stuck to his morals and training and was usually proven right. His quiet strength and unwavering dedication to victims—such as the moment when he risked his career and medical license by administering the illegal substance Ibogaine to help a teen overcome heroin addiction—made him a beloved figure among his peers and fans alike.

Huang wouldn't have had the same impact without BD Wong—a groundbreaking actor known for *Jurassic Park*, *Mr. Robot*, *Mulan*, and his Tony-winning role in *M. Butterfly* that made him the only actor to win a Tony, Drama Desk, Outer Critics Circle, Clarence Derwent, and Theatre World Award for the same role. A real-life civil rights advocate, Wong revealed that Huang's late-in-the-series coming out felt a bit like a shortcut, but he remains proud of offering the on-screen representation of a positive Asian and gay character that he lacked as a child. Any episode with Huang promised to be top-tier *SVU*.

DR. MELINDA WARNER

PORTRAYED BY: Tamara Tunie

FIRST APPEARANCE: "Noncompliance" (S2, E6; 2000)

LAST APPEARANCE: "The Five Hundredth Episode" (S23, E6; 2021)

Growing up, actress Tamara Tunie's parents were both morticians and the family lived above the funeral parlor. This unique childhood meant that Tunie was completely comfortable around death, though her friends were initially hesitant to come over and play. Her family continues to operate the funeral home in suburban Pittsburgh. Talk about art imitating life!

404

No one delivers complex expository technojargon quite like Dr. Melinda Warner, *SVU*'s steadfast medical examiner and the only ME in show history to be in the main credits. She spoke for the dead and helped to bring them vengeance, seamlessly combining warmth and precision with every diagnosis. After joining the show in Season 2 as a recurring character, Warner had become a series regular by Season 7, thanks to her expert knowledge and infectious personality.

The role of a medical examiner on crime procedurals is often limited to explaining DNA results or determining the cause of death. Warner stood out by breaking down dense science in a way both the detectives and audience could understand. Yet she wasn't just about facts; Warner connected with the squad, offering quiet moments of compassion—like comforting Benson after her traumatic undercover stint in prison—and even flirting with Fin from time to time. As a Gulf War veteran and former Air Force doctor, Warner brought a unique blend of expertise and military precision to the job, and when she single-handedly took down a kidnapper, proved she could handle pressure anywhere. But that didn't mean she never contributed funny one-liners after doing an autopsy. After all, in a job that deals with corpses daily, a little levity is necessary.

Tamara Tunie brought strength, reliability, and much-needed representation as a woman of color in a high-ranking scientific role. She showed that to find justice, you need knowledge. And thankfully for Benson, Stabler, Fin, Munch, and the rest, Warner possessed enough for all of them.

ROMANCING ♥ THE SQUAD

Detectives need love too! Romance and heartbreak have always been part of *SVU*'s DNA, but for Benson, love has taken a back seat to work.

Here's a rundown of the squad's most memorable romances:

OLIVIA BENSON

- Brian Cassidy: **A one-night stand turned rekindled romance that ended with conflicting goals. Played by Dean Winters.**
- Kurt Moss: **A brief romance derailed by professional ethics. Played by Bill Pullman.**
- David Haden: **A promising relationship cut short to protect the integrity of the SVU and avoid conflicts at work. Played by Harry Connick Jr.**
- Ed Tucker: **Her most mature relationship, but Benson wasn't ready to retire alongside him. Played by Robert John Burke.**
- Burton Lowe: **A former fiancé later revealed as a serial predator—she didn't get a ring, but he got the cuffs. Played by Aidan Quinn.**
- Trevor Langan: **Defense attorney who once took Benson to a gala. Played by Peter Hermann (real-life husband of Mariska Hargitay).**
- Elliot Stabler: **Decades of chemistry. Unresolved tension. A necklace. An almost kiss. Endgame? You never know! Played by Christopher Meloni.**

AMANDA ROLLINS

- Nick Amaro: **Hinted-at romance that fizzled out. Played by Danny Pino.**

- Dominick Carisi, Jr.: **A fan-favorite slow-burn that blossomed into marriage. Played by Peter Scanavino.**

FIN TUTUOLA

- Teresa Randall: **Ex-wife that reappeared at various points. Mother to Ken Randall and his half-brother Darius Parker. Played by LisaGay Hamilton.**
- Phoebe Baker: **Former partner turned rekindled romance. They're happy together without marriage. Played by Jennifer Esposito.**

ELLIOT STABLER

- Kathy Stabler: **High school sweetheart and wife until her tragic death. Played by Isabel Gillies.**
- Dani Beck: **Just a kiss . . . but what a kiss. Played by Connie Nielsen.**

- Dr. Rebecca Hendrix: **A cop-turned-shrink whose flirty exchanges clearly made Benson jealous. Played by Mary Stuart Masterson.**
- Olivia Benson: ***We've already said enough.***

JOHN MUNCH

- Gwen Munch: **The only one of John Munch's ex-wives to appear on-screen, whose mental health challenges ended their marriage. Played by Carol Kane.**

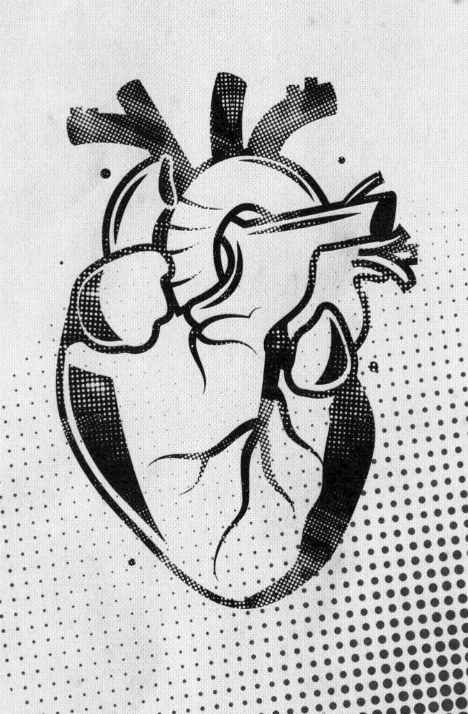

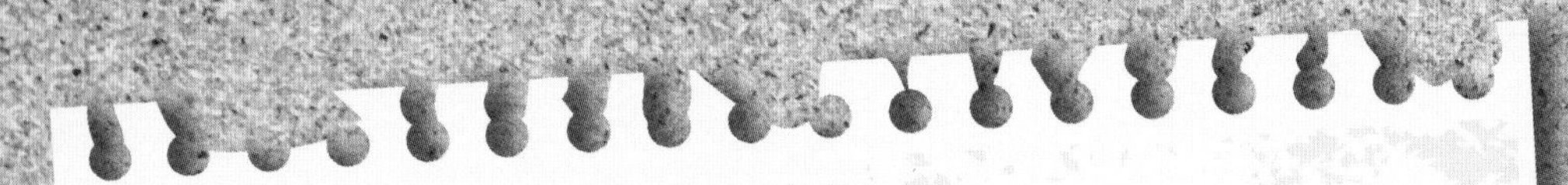

ADA ALEXANDRA "ALEX" CABOT

PORTRAYED BY: Stephanie March

FIRST APPEARANCE: "Wrong Is Right" (S2, E1; 2000)

LAST APPEARANCE: "Sunk Cost Fallacy" (S19, E19; 2018)

With unwavering resolve and razor-sharp instincts, Alex Cabot wasn't just another prosecutor. As *SVU*'s first full-time ADA, this Harvard grad brought a sharp mind, unshakeable tenacity, and a surprising sense of humor to the job. (To prepare for her role, March shadowed real-life prosecutor Linda Fairstein, learning how gallows humor helps DAs cope with the intense work.) Cabot exuded poise, intelligence, confidence, and elegance: the epitome of professionalism. Her signature accessory? Glasses, which March jokingly dubbed "the glasses of justice." When she started, March couldn't wear contacts and suggested to Dick Wolf that her character don glasses for a bookish edge. She was already lawyering her way through production even then.

Superfans have often speculated on a romantic connection between Cabot and Benson. Showrunner Neal Baer even acknowledged the subtext: "We read the fan sites. All the codes are in there." And fans were stunned when Cabot left the show in Season 5 by faking her own death to enter witness protection. She would return sporadically through Season 19, revealing a softer side as she reflected on her manufactured life in Wisconsin under the alias "Emily." Cabot's role ultimately shifted to vigilante as she began helping battered women escape their abusers. That dedication extended off-screen when March became an advocate for survivors of sexual violence, serving on the board of the Panzi Foundation in the Democratic Republic of Congo. Even in real life, Cabot's spirit lives on: relentless, fearless, and always fighting for victims.

ADA CASEY NOVAK

PORTRAYED BY: Diane Neal

FIRST APPEARANCE: “Serendipity” (S5, E5; 2003)

LAST APPEARANCE: “Valentine’s Day” (S13, E18; 2012)

Diane Neal, a survivor of sexual assault, has spoken openly about her experience and the importance of advocacy. Her work with Denim Day, a campaign raising awareness about sexual violence, reflects her commitment to helping survivors. Denim Day takes place on the last Wednesday of April during Sexual Assault Awareness Month. Learn more at denimdayinfo.org.

In Season 5, Casey Novak's unforgettable debut signaled a tonal shift for *SVU*'s ADA, because rather than confining herself to offices and courtrooms, she had no problem getting down and dirty in the field. What truly humanized her was a vulnerable conversation with District Attorney Arthur Branch in her first episode where she expressed doubts about handling the job. Branch assured her that she passed his "test" with flying colors.

Novak admirably took on corrupt judges, interrupted poker games to get warrants, and literally went toe-to-toe with the Pentagon. Fans also saw her tough exterior crack when the emotional toll of her work caught up with her, such as the moment when a traumatized Novak broke down in Benson's arms after being brutally attacked. Diane Neal shaped her character as a tomboy with a working-class background who only wore heels when absolutely necessary—a trait Neal herself shared. Her most famous wardrobe piece? The *Sex Crimes* softball T-shirt from the episode "Night," (S6, E20; 2005) something writer Amanda Green (a former cop) confirmed was based on the real Brooklyn SVU team's jerseys.

A Virginia-born newcomer to acting, Neal dabbled in archeology, ice skating, and modeling before she landed her most iconic role. Over 5 seasons and 113 episodes, Casey Novak became a cornerstone of *SVU*.
With sass, style, and epic takedowns, she was unafraid of those who stood in her way.
Just ask any of the hardened criminals that contributed to her 71 percent conviction rate.
Fans don't just like Novak's work, they love it.

ADA RAFAEL BARBA

PORTRAYED BY: Raúl Esparza

FIRST APPEARANCE: "Twenty-Five Acts" (S14, E3; 2012)

LAST APPEARANCE: "A Final Call at Forlini's Bar" (S23, E22; 2022)

Another ADA with a remarkable entrance, Rafael Barba's first appearance was one of the boldest in *SVU* history. While prosecuting talk show host Adam Cain for rape, Barba didn't rely on legalese to win over the jury. Instead, he took a belt, gave it to Cain, and taunted him into choking him in open court—exposing Cain's violent tendencies on the spot. Message received: there was a new ADA in town.

Like his flashy tailored suits, suspenders, and pocket squares (all intentional choices by Broadway actor Raúl Esparza), he was sharp, precise, and looked good inside and outside of the courtroom. His direct approach to the law, larger-than-life presence, and flair for the dramatic made him a fan favorite, while his biting sarcasm, quick wit, and frequent legal putdowns of Carisi elevated the show. At the heart of Barba's tenure was his close relationship with Benson. She affectionately nicknamed him "Rafa," and some fans saw potential for a deeper connection. His mother said Benson drove him crazy . . . maybe crazy in love? For now, we'll have to remain content with them being close friends.

True to form, Barba left the show dramatically—and in a way that revealed his emotional depth. In one of the show's most controversial moments, he made the gut-wrenching decision to disconnect life support for a vegetative infant, something he regretted not doing for his own father. This powerfully complex choice led to his resignation and divided fans while adding layers to his character. Barba's tough exterior and life lessons from his Bronx roots and Harvard Law informed the man who became one of *SVU*'s best ADAs.

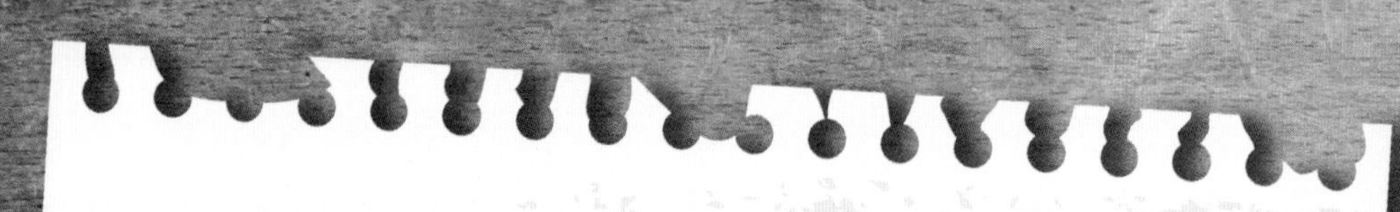

DETECTIVE NICK AMARO

PORTRAYED BY: Danny Pino

FIRST APPEARANCE: "Scorched Earth" (S13, E1; 2011)

LAST APPEARANCE: "The Five Hundredth Episode" (S23, E6; 2021)

After Stabler's departure, *SVU* faced a seismic shift. Benson needed a new partner until she could take center stage. Enter: Nick Amaro. Played brilliantly by Danny Pino, Amaro brought Cuban-Italian heritage, a complex backstory, and dare we say, dashing good looks to the precinct. Like Stabler, he had a temper, but while Stabler exploded, Amaro simmered until he boiled over. His demons stemmed from an abusive childhood and a strained marriage to his wife Maria (Laura Benanti), and his personal struggles bled into his deep investment in his work. His father, Nicolas Amaro Sr. (Armand Assante), loomed large, inspiring Amaro's protectiveness of women and children and his zero-tolerance stance on domestic violence.

One notable aspect of his character was his antagonistic relationship with ADA Rafael Barba, marked by sharp exchanges like their memorable elevator confrontation. Despite the tension, their relationship evolved, softening over time. He had a similarly notable—and notably flirtatious—relationship with Detective Rollins, with writers leaving their attraction ambiguous but undeniable until Rollins met Carisi.

Despite Amaro's flaws, he grew. Yes, he was impulsive, but he cared too much to give less than everything he had. His NYPD career ended after a courtroom shootout left him injured and he decided to retire to focus on his family. His SVU story seemed over until the landmark five hundredth episode revealed he was solving cold cases as a geneticist—still fighting for justice, but with far less risk of needing to rough up perps.

DETECTIVE / ADA DOMINICK "SONNY" CARISI JR.

PORTRAYED BY: Peter Scanavino

FIRST APPEARANCE: "Girls Disappeared" (S16, E1; 2014)

When Amaro was temporarily out of commission, Dominick Carisi, Jr. showed up like a Staten Island guardian angel. With his thick accent, brash, boisterous demeanor, blue-collar charm, and a thankfully short-lived '70s stache, Carisi was a standout, and initially divisive, figure. But his unshakeable drive and big heart quickly won everyone over. Known for his interrogation skills, he could empathize with suspects (or pretend to) and always had his partners' backs in the field.

Faith and family have always shaped Carisi's life. He has three *very* Italian sisters, devout Catholic parents, and once considered the priesthood before choosing the NYPD. Cases involving religious leaders who abuse authority particularly enrage him. With a love for vests, his wardrobe has evolved over time from frumpy suits to designer duds and a polished salt-and-pepper hairstyle. His most compelling personal arc has been his romance with Rollins, as their relationship grew from playful banter to courthouse marriage to godmother Olivia Benson baptizing their first child.

But perhaps Carisi's most important journey was studying to become *SVU*'s next great ADA. While taking night classes at Fordham Law, he learned the ropes from reluctant mentor ADA Rafael Barba. Their frequent quick-witted jousts became fan favorites, and in Season 21, after five years with the SVU, Carisi joined the DA's office. In Season 22 he finally bested Barba in court—and ADA Carisi truly arrived.

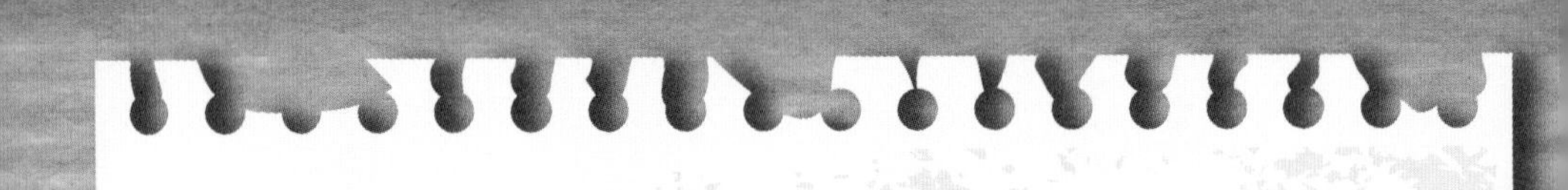

DETECTIVE AMANDA ROLLINS

PORTRAYED BY: Kelli Giddish

FIRST APPEARANCE: “Scorched Earth” (S13, E1; 2011)

Joining *SVU* in a dynamic one-two punch alongside Detective Nick Amaro, Detective Amanda Rollins brought an undeniable spark to the squad room. She evolved into one of the show's most complex and beloved characters whose personal struggles captured viewers' hearts.

Hailing from Loganville, Georgia, Rollins grew up in a troubled and chaotic family. Despite her hardships, she joined the Atlanta PD before transferring to the Manhattan SVU. Her Southern roots (shared by actress Kelli Giddish, also from Georgia) are reflected in her accent and Easter eggs like Atlanta Braves memorabilia and the taxidermized chipmunk on her desk. Behind the scenes, this fuzzy companion was nicknamed "DC" (Dead Chipmunk) by Ice-T. Even Rollins's dog, Frannie Mae, who once helped chase down William Lewis, belongs to Giddish in real life.

Captain Cragen proved pivotal in Rollins's early days, helping her confront her gambling addiction by getting her help rather than dismissing her. This raw, complex storyline added much-needed grit during the show's transitional period after Stabler's departure. Fans love her blunt, hard-edged attitude. She doesn't sugarcoat anything and doesn't like fortune cookie philosophy. Her darkest moment came when revealing she'd been sexually assaulted by Deputy Chief Patton in Atlanta—a trauma that shaped her empathy for victims. Rollins's most important relationship is with Sonny Carisi Jr.—the perfect example of a "golden retriever boyfriend and black cat girlfriend," dubbed "Rollisi" by fans. Rollins's evolution from flawed detective to confident, fulfilled woman resonated with fans. It's hard to imagine *SVU* without Rollins's brand of toughness. And thankfully, we don't have to.

DETECTIVE BRIAN CASSIDY

PORTRAYED BY: Dean Winters

FIRST APPEARANCE: "Payback" (S1, E1; 1999)

LAST APPEARANCE: "Facing Demons" (S20, E16; 2019)

THE RETURN OF CASSIDY

Winters told The A.V. Club that at 5 a.m. one morning, he heard a film crew outside his apartment and, like a true New Yorker, yelled out the window. The voice yelling back? Richard Belzer. Curious, Winters went down and found the *SVU* cast filming in front of his building. "One thing led to another and the next week, I was back as a guest star." Now that's a classic *SVU* twist.

Detective Brian Cassidy was the first *SVU* cast member to leave the show (after only thirteen episodes), but his journey on the program was marked by growth, struggle, and emotional revelations. Initially he was a naive rookie; a bull in a china shop clearly ill-equipped for the emotional toll of investigating sex crimes. Partnered with John Munch, he was eager to prove himself, but his inexperience and hotheaded nature often led to clashes with colleagues. But what ultimately sealed his fate was a lack of professional detachment; Cragen transferred him to Narcotics after Cassidy failed to cope with a visit to a rape survivor. In real life, actor Dean Winters left the show because of his commitments to a role on HBO's *Oz*. Before his departure, Cassidy shared a memorable fling with Benson—the first time we saw her romantically involved with anyone.

Years later, Cassidy made a surprise return in Season 13, undercover in a high-stakes operation. He had grown into a hardened investigator—scarred but wiser. He rekindled his romance with Benson, but they ultimately parted ways, realizing they wanted different things in life. His later appearances revealed a heartbreaking story: Cassidy had been molested by his Little League coach as a child, a secret that had haunted him for years and likely explained his behavior in Season 1. Whether this was retroactively fixing a problem or not, it helped humanize Cassidy. With Benson's support, he testified against his abuser, bringing his story full circle. His return wasn't just a cameo—it was a real story of redemption.

DETECTIVE MONIQUE JEFFRIES

PORTRAYED BY: Michelle Hurd

FIRST APPEARANCE: "Payback" (S1, E1; 1999)

LAST APPEARANCE: "Runaway" (S2, E16; 2001)

Though Detective Monique Jeffries was an original *SVU* cast member, she was also one of the first to leave the show. A tough, street-smart detective, Jeffries partnered with several colleagues, including Brian Cassidy, Ken Briscoe (nephew of *Law & Order*'s Lennie Briscoe), and later John Munch, with whom she shared sharp banter and occasional clashes. But it was her dramatic departure that left a lasting impression.

Jeffries's story arc took a dark turn after she survived a near-death experience. Traumatized but exhilarated, she spiraled emotionally until she was reassigned to desk work, with her ultimate exit unfolding in waves. Her final appearance confused viewers, as it seemed like she had rejoined the squad; in reality, that episode was filmed before her departure but was aired later. Behind the scenes, Hurd left the show due to frustrations over her character's limited development. Dick Wolf promised a bigger arc, but it never materialized. Producers preferred Benson and Stabler as the only mixed-gender duo, and Hurd accepted an offer to join Showtime's *Leap Years*. Despite all this, Hurd has no hard feelings and remains open to returning—imagining Jeffries as a judge or district attorney.

Fans remain divided on Jeffries's exit. Some argue that her dismissal was unwarranted considering the leniency shown to characters like Rollins, whose personal struggles complicate her work, or Stabler, whose volatility has caused countless problems. Others feel her story reflects the double standards women and people of color face—an issue that still resonates. And without Jeffries moving on, we would never have gotten Fin. Perhaps it's finally time for a reunion.

RECURRING CHARACTERS

SISTER PEG

PORTRAYED BY: Charlayne Woodard

FIRST APPEARANCE: "Silence" (S3, E23; 2002)

LAST APPEARANCE: "Smoked" (S12, E24; 2011)

When a character only appears in eight episodes, it's easy to forget them. But not Sister Peg. As a Catholic nun and beacon of compassion for New York's most vulnerable, Sister Peg dedicated her life to supporting sex workers, the homeless, and drug addicts as if they were family. She ran a mobile health unit and handed out clean needles and contraception to promote safe sex, and her pragmatic approach made her a trusted ally to Benson and Stabler, who often turned to her for street intel. But she wasn't your typical nun—instead of wearing a habit, she wore her heart on her sleeve. Despite her brief screen time, fans continue to celebrate her empathetic demeanor, unflappable resolve, and practical approach to tackling systemic problems.

But in "Smoked" (S12, E24; 2011), Sister Peg is suddenly killed, a fate that many fans saw as unnecessary shock value. Tony-nominated actress Charlayne Woodard fittingly described her character as a woman who "saw her community and decided to serve." That sums it up perfectly.

WILLIAM DODDS

PORTRAYED BY: PETER GALLAGHER

FIRST APPEARANCE: "HOLDEN'S MANIFESTO" (S16, E4; 2014)

LAST APPEARANCE: "I'M GOING TO MAKE YOU A STAR" (S21, E1; 2019)

Few *SVU* characters have walked the fine line between antagonist and ally as deftly as Deputy Chief William Dodds. Of course, it helps when they're portrayed by Peter Gallagher, whose twitch of an eyebrow or steely glance could reduce anyone to a puddle. Dodds was relentless in demanding results, often clashing with Benson over his impossibly high standards. But beneath the thousand-dollar suits was a man devoted to both justice and family—especially his son, Sergeant Mike Dodds, who joined the SVU (as Benson's second-in-command when she was promoted to Lieutenant) at his father's encouragement at the beginning of Season 17.

When Mike was killed in the line of duty, the squad was deeply affected and Dodds gradually shed the hardened exterior he often wore like one of his suits. His tenure would conclude in Season 21 after he became the fall guy for a high-profile case that ruffled the NYPD brass. After agreeing to be demoted and transferred to Staten Island's Traffic and Safety Task Force, Dodds surprised Benson by telling her that he made her promotion to captain a part of his deal. In a touching farewell, he offered her a heartfelt toast to her future success. It was a fitting end for Dodds—and a fitting beginning for Benson.

ELIZABETH DONNELLY

PORTRAYED BY: Judith Light

FIRST APPEARANCE: "Guilt" (S3, E18; 2002)

LAST APPEARANCE: "Behave" (S12, E3; 2010)

Fearless. Unapologetic. Ballsy. Bureau Chief ADA-turned-Judge Elizabeth Donnelly, played by the legendary Judith Light, was a force to be reckoned with. Tough but fair, Donnelly had zero tolerance for sloppy detection, always making the prosecution work to prove their case. Integrity was her cornerstone, and she held everyone—including herself—accountable. Fans still rave about her fiery wit and no-nonsense commands. From flirting with Stabler on her doorstep (in a robe, no less) to fiercely defending him and Novak in court, Donnelly was arguably *SVU*'s best judge. But her most compelling dynamic? Trading barbs and wisdom with ADA Alex Cabot (Stephanie March). Off-screen, Light and March bonded over the societal pressures of being childless women, with Light, much like Donnelly, summing up life without kids perfectly: "Let me tell you something about people who don't have children: We're fine." Producer Ted Kotcheff created Donnelly specifically for Light after seeing her in a play. And for that, all we can say is . . . thank you, Ted.

THE SCENE OF THE CAMEO

Did you know some of *SVU*'s most beloved stars appeared on the show as entirely different characters *before* becoming recurring favorites we know and love? From one-off suspects to shady criminals—and even a crooked cop—these early performances helped fast-track their path to primetime!

DIANE NEAL (ADA CASEY NOVAK)
Two years before she became ADA, Neal played Amelia Chase, a stockbroker complicit in the rape of a male stripper in "Ridicule" (S3, E10; 2001).

KELLI GIDDISH (DETECTIVE AMANDA ROLLINS)
In "Outsider" (S8, E12; 2007), Giddish gives a brief but powerful performance as socialite Kara Bawson, a rape victim interviewed by Fin as the team investigates a serial rapist.

KEVIN KANE (DETECTIVE TERRY BRUNO)
Kane portrayed four separate *SVU* minor characters—a murderer in "Inconceivable" (S9, E14; 2008); an officer in "Child's Welfare" (S13, E16; 2012); a major in "Nationwide Manhunt" (S17, E14; 2016); and the husband of a victim in "Mea Culpa" (S20, E9; 2018). Talk about paying your dues!

TERRY SERPICO (CHIEF TOMMY McGRATH)
The king of cameos! Serpico has played *nine* different minor characters across all *Law & Order* shows. On *SVU* he was a petty criminal in "Closure (Part I)" (S1, E10; 2000); a corrupt cop in "Rotten" (S4, E13; 2003); a pedophile and murderer in "Quarry" (S6, E13; 2005); and a power-hungry rapist in "Military Justice" (S15, E8; 2013).

DECLAN MURPHY

PORTRAYED BY: Donal Logue

FIRST APPEARANCE: "Gambler's Fallacy" (S15, E17; 2014)

LAST APPEARANCE: "Silent Night, Hateful Night" (S23, E10; 2022)

As one of *SVU*'s most enigmatic and mysterious characters, Captain Declan Murphy first appeared as undercover crime boss Declan O'Rourke, testing Rollins's loyalty during her gambling crisis and revealing his willingness to walk in morally gray areas for justice. Murphy's biggest moment came in "Beast's Obsession" (S15, E20; 2014), when he became Acting Captain during William Lewis's escape. His tactical expertise and growing respect for Benson stood out—especially when he ordered twenty-four-hour security for her, which, of course, she ignored. Personally, he packed the biggest punch when it was revealed that he was the father of Rollins's daughter, Jesse. Despite undercover work often pulling him away, he tried to reconnect with Rollins and Jesse, torn between duty and regret, and thanks to Donal Logue's depth and charm, Murphy was a character you wanted to believe in. And while some might knock him for talking in the third person, there's no denying Logue, with his vast film and TV experience before joining *SVU*, brought a seasoned intensity that sharpened the team's on-screen dynamic.

NOAH PORTER BENSON

PORTRAYED BY: Ryan Buggle (current), Jack Nawada-Braunwart, Bradley Dubow, Skyler Dubow

FIRST APPEARANCE: "Wednesday's Child" (S15, E14; 2014)

Noah Porter Benson had a tragic start. Born to Ellie Porter, a sex worker, his early life was filled with trauma in the form of foster care, the loss of his biological mother, and an uncertain future. But after discovering him in a motel room during a child pornography bust with Rollins, Benson stepped in, gaining temporary custody and later adopting him. His journey hasn't been easy—this is *SVU*, after all! But credit goes to Lucy Huston (played by Bronwyn Reed), Noah's nanny and the true unsung hero of his development.

One of Noah's most intense storylines has been a custody battle with his biological grandmother, Sheila Porter (played by Mariska Hargitay's real-life friend, Brooke Shields), which included a tense kidnapping and an unforgettable showdown. And in Season 23, Noah made *SVU* history by coming out as bisexual—the youngest LGBTQIA+ character in the franchise. Hargitay called actor Ryan Buggle (who has grown up alongside his character; a rarity in TV) "wise beyond his years," with Buggle in turn calling Hargitay, "a dream." Fans have mixed reactions to Noah. Some love the emotional depth he adds to the show, while others feel his storylines distract from the main cases. But love him or not, his character clearly proves that chosen family can be just as powerful as any we're born into.

ED TUCKER

PORTRAYED BY: Robert John Burke

FIRST APPEARANCE: "Counterfeit"
(S3, E14; 2002)

LAST APPEARANCE: "The Longest Night of Rain"
(S21, E12; 2020)

Ed Tucker's job as Internal Affairs Bureau (IAB) Captain, played brilliantly by Robert John Burke, was simple but thankless: root out misconduct, confront corruption, and keep cops in line—whether they liked him or not. For most of his tenure, Tucker clashed with the SVU detectives. Then, his romance with Benson transformed him from adversary to a more human and layered character. Though they meshed well together as fellow workaholics, with Tucker offering Benson rare peace outside of their demanding jobs, the relationship ended in "Chasing Theo" (S18, E8; 2017) when Tucker revealed he was considering retirement—something Benson couldn't imagine for herself.

Years later, Benson learns that Tucker had married someone else, and that he was diagnosed with terminal brain cancer, likely caused by exposure to Ground Zero on 9/11. Tucker would ultimately face his fate with unflinching practicality, choosing to end his own life rather than burden his wife with years of caregiving. While some fans saw his suicide as unnecessary, it underscored *SVU*'s ability to tackle heavy issues, especially those that affect police forces in real life.

RYAN O'HALLORAN

PORTRAYED BY: Mike Doyle

FIRST APPEARANCE: "Choice" (S5, E7; 2003)

LAST APPEARANCE: "Zebras" (S10, E22; 2009)

Ryan O'Halloran, a steady hand in the crime lab, delivered expert forensic evidence in over fifty episodes—second only to Noah Porter Benson for most appearances by a recurring character. Methodical and professional, O'Halloran was an approachable asset whose findings, whether reconstructing fragmented evidence or uncovering patterns, always unearthed the smoking gun.

O'Halloran's heroics were tragically cut short by a shocking death at the hands of fellow technician Dale Stuckey. While he wasn't a lead, his death still stings thanks to Mike Doyle's likeable and understated performance. Doyle described *SVU*'s set as one of the funniest ever, thanks to Mariska Hargitay and Christopher Meloni's constant antics. Showrunner Neal Baer reassured Doyle his exit wasn't due to disliking the character—he simply wanted O'Halloran to go out with a bang. Or maybe a bing, bang, bong. Still too soon?

RUBEN MORALES

PORTRAYED BY: Joel de la Fuente

FIRST APPEARANCE: "Surveillance"
(S3, E17; 2002)

LAST APPEARANCE: "Bully" (S12, E18; 2011)

As the backbone of the Technical Assistance Response Unit (TARU), Ruben Morales was a wizard with corrupted audio, grainy surveillance footage, and triangulating locations of suspects from weak cell signals, especially under immense pressure. It didn't matter if the sample was wet, burned, or broken—he would fix it. Morales was calm but precise, and that made him indispensable. Surprisingly for a smaller recurring character, fans rejoiced when Morales got his own B-storyline in "Web" (S7, E21; 2006), which revealed a heartbreaking story of regret.

When actor de la Fuente was being cast, he auditioned for Forensics Technician Burt Trevor—a role that ultimately went to Daniel Sunjata, who debuted in "Prodigy" (S3, E13; 2002) and portrayed the character for fifteen episodes over three seasons before leaving to join the cast of *Rescue Me*. De la Fuente impressed the producers enough that they created a new character for him: Ruben Morales, who made his first appearance just three episodes later. While de la Fuente was used to playing Hispanic or Asian characters of undetermined origin (he is Filipino himself) the show decided to adapt the character's name to match his ethnicity, which was a rare and thoughtful touch for him and for the show's overall representation in early 2000s TV.

CHESTER LAKE

PORTRAYED BY: Adam Beach

FIRST APPEARANCE: "Outsider" (S8, E12; 2007)

LAST APPEARANCE: "Cold" (S9, E19; 2008)

Detective Chester Lake joined the squad as a main cast member in Season 9 after transferring from Brooklyn's SVU. A Native American of Mohawk descent, Lake brought a fresh perspective with his heritage, his family's legacy as ironworkers, his past in the foster system, and his experience as an MMA fighter nicknamed "Naptime." Suffering from insomnia, his late-night walks gave him a brooding vibe, much like the hard-nosed detectives of yesteryear. But Lake wasn't without comedic moments. In "Savant," (S9, E4; 2007), he affectionately puts his hand on Fin's leg when they're mistaken for a gay couple. Ice-T's reaction? Priceless.

Lake only lasted one season (showrunner Neal Baer wanted to refocus on the core cast) but his exit was anything but boring as he was arrested for murder after shooting a fellow officer. Beach viewed the role as groundbreaking for Native American representation on TV and believed that it opened the doors for more inclusivity in Hollywood. Wrong fit for the show? Underused and underrated? Character assassination from the writers? That's for you to decide. But while his time on the show may have been brief, Adam Beach sure made it count.

DANI BECK

PORTRAYED BY: Connie Nielsen

FIRST APPEARANCE: "Clock" (S8, E2; 2006)

LAST APPEARANCE: "Cage" (S8, E8; 2006)

Detective Dani Beck temporarily joined the SVU while Benson went deep undercover as "Persephone James" with an ecoterrorist group (and in one scene, wakes up from being knocked out by moaning Elliot's name in a hospital)—in actuality, it was Mariska Hargitay's maternity leave that made way for the squad's new addition.

Beck was a driven Warrants Squad detective shaped by the loss of her husband (an NYPD officer killed in the line of duty), whose impulsive style often clashed with the team, practically creating two Stablers. The palpable tension between her and Stabler even led to a kiss. Beck's standout moment came in "Recall" (S8, E3; 2006), when she comforted an assault victim (Leslie Caron, who won an Emmy for her role) in French. In the following episode, Nielsen reunited with actor Jerry Lewis, her costar from her film debut, *Par où t'es rentré? On t'a pas vu sortir* (1984). Off-screen, Nielsen—who had risen to stardom in *Gladiator* (2000)—revealed that the demanding filming schedule of a TV show (and mixed fan reception to her character and performance) discouraged her from reprising the role.

SHEAR PANIC

Over the years, all of the characters have developed unique and iconic styles, but in Season 3, Olivia Benson's pixie cut almost cost Mariska Hargitay her job! While in the middle of filming an episode, Hargitay decided to get a trim for a photoshoot. After she gave the stylist a glass of wine, he accidentally snipped the wrong piece. When the dailies came in, the producers weren't happy, and series creator Dick Wolf told her, "I've fired people for less." Thankfully for Mariska (and *SVU* fans everywhere) she smoothed things over, and Olivia Benson lived to see another day.

NEW KIDS ON THE BEAT

With fresh faces and an ever-changing dynamic, these recently introduced characters ensure that the squad room always feels new—even if some don't stick around for long.

CAPTAIN RENEE CURRY
(played by Aimé Donna Kelly)

A former IAB Captain turned member of the SVU, Curry's debut had her investigating Benson and Fin about a lawsuit. She has sharp instincts, surprisingly good baking skills, and has been involved in several high-stakes cases, like finding McGrath's daughter's rapist.

DETECTIVE JOSE "JOE" VELASCO
(played by Octavio Pisano)

Velasco is a resilient, relentless, street-smart investigator from Ciudad Juárez, Mexico, with a complicated past and serious undercover skills. His rough upbringing and history of survival make him a fierce protector, but his methods occasionally blur the lines of justice and vengeance. Once Velasco earned Benson's trust, he became a standout member of the team.

DETECTIVE TERRY BRUNO
(played by Kevin Kane)

A Bronx SVU transfer with a checkered past, Bruno got a second chance after blowing the whistle on NYPD corruption. With a knack for comedic relief, Bruno is known for his professionalism and surprisingly enviable collection of high-end watches.

DETECTIVE KATE SILVA

(played by Juliana Aidén Martinez)

Ambitious and quick on her feet, Silva comes from Brooklyn's Homicide Division and has deep NYPD roots through her father. Tough, smart, and already a rising star, the only question that remains is *why* she asked to be transferred to the SVU.

DETECTIVE GRACE MUNCY

(played by Molly Burnett)

Formerly with the Bronx Gang Unit, Muncy struggled to fit in initially, despite her empathy and no-nonsense approach. She bonded with Velasco before transferring to a DEA (Drug Enforcement Agency) task force.

DETECTIVE KATRIONA "KAT" TAMIN

(played by Jamie Gray Hyder)

A Vice Squad transfer, Tamin was the show's first openly LGBTQIA+ detective and always had her case closure rate top of mind. After being shot in the line of duty, she decided the intensity of the SVU was too much and left to help victims in other ways.

DEPUTY MAYOR CHRISTIAN GARLAND

(played by Demore Barnes)

As former Deputy Chief of the SVU, Garland often clashed with bureaucracy, but his calm demeanor and thoughtful approach to leadership earned him respect. His departure after eighteen episodes disappointed fans (and Barnes), but Garland has the distinction of being the first Black Deputy Chief on *SVU* and the only Deputy Chief in the *Law & Order* franchise to star as a main cast member.

156 LASALLE
K915

THE CASE FILES

ADD TO WATCHLIST

With over twenty-five seasons, *SVU* has delivered some of the most gripping and unforgettable episodes in TV history. But with nearly six hundred episodes, even the most seasoned detectives would agree . . . that's a lot of TV to sift through! Sure, it's the perfect binge-worthy show, but for a new viewer or someone short on time, where do you even begin?

The beauty of a crime procedural is that you can dive in almost anywhere and still get the full experience. These shows are always in syndication (a.k.a. reruns) because you never need to catch them in order. So, whether you're a newbie giving this show a first look or a die-hard needing a palette cleanser, this shortlist of essential episodes, presented in order of release and by no means definitive, will have you locked and loaded for the full *SVU* experience.

"COUNTDOWN" (S2, E15; 2001)

Written By: Dawn DeNoon & Lisa Marie Petersen
Directed By: Steve Shill

In one of the most heart-pounding challenges the SVU team faced early in the series, the squad has only seventy-two hours to locate a serial predator who has kidnapped, raped, and murdered four young girls. With the clock literally ticking, the detectives must prevent the latest victim from meeting the same horrifying fate.

WHY IT'S ICONIC: "Countdown" stands out for its intense pacing and innovative structure, which mirrors the real-time urgency of the show *24*. The episode also highlights *SVU*'s knack for casting comedic actors in creepy roles, with Jim Gaffigan delivering an unforgettable cameo performance as a pedophile and former children's birthday clown.

CASE FILES: This episode's villain, Clayton Mills (Jonathan Fried), was inspired by real-life serial killers such as Gary Ridgway (the Green River Killer), who avoided the death penalty by revealing information about his victims.

WRAP SHEET: This episode is the only one in *SVU* history to feature interstitial scene cards with ticking seconds, emphasizing the urgency of the case and elevating the tension. This stylistic choice was groundbreaking for the series and remains a unique hallmark of the episode.

"LOSS" (S5, E4; 2003)

Written By: Tara Butters & Michele Fazekas
Directed By: Constantine Makris

When an undercover DEA agent is brutally raped and murdered, Benson and Stabler uncover a dangerous connection to the Colombian drug cartel. ADA Alex Cabot is at the heart of the case, which puts her directly in the cartel's crosshairs.

WHY IT'S ICONIC: Few other *SVU* episodes match the hard-hitting weight of the emotional "farewell" to beloved character Alex Cabot. This was a defining episode for actress Stephanie March, whose performance captured her vulnerability and left fans on the edge of their seats.

CASE FILES: After first leaving the show, March got a call from Dick Wolf to star in a new spin-off, *Conviction* (2006), where she would reprise her role as Alexandra Cabot and become Bureau Chief ADA overseeing young prosecutors. Despite Dick Wolf's attempts at making this new show a "charactercedural" (focusing on characters' personal lives over cases), the show struggled against CBS's *Numb3rs* and was canceled after just thirteen episodes.

WRAP SHEET: March's *SVU* experience didn't just inspire her advocacy off-camera; it also led to the creation of her beauty brand, SheSpoke, which she cofounded with former *SVU* makeup artist and current Makeup Department Head at *Organized Crime*, Rebecca Perkins.

"MEAN" (S5, E17; 2004)

Written By: Tara Butters & Michele Fazekas
Directed By: Constantine Makris

Teenager Emily Sullivan is found murdered in a car trunk, leading to an investigation that reveals a chilling world of secrets, cruelty, and betrayal amongst her own friends. Stabler likens the girls' clique to the mafia with their unspoken code of silence, which results in a trial full of fireworks.

WHY IT'S ICONIC: Few episodes tackle the complexities of being a teenager and how cruel your peers can be as powerfully as "Mean." The case highlights the devastating impact of bullying, toxic friendships, and peer pressure.

CASE FILES: This episode draws inspiration from the 1992 murder of twelve-year-old Shanda Sharer at the hands of four teenage girls in Madison, Indiana that shocked the nation.

WRAP SHEET: Actress Kelli Garner (head mean girl Brittany O'Malley) revealed on *That's Messed Up: An SVU Podcast* that Dann Florek (Cragen) was her favorite cast member. She credits him with boosting her confidence during their interrogation scenes and says, to this day, his reassuring voice still echoes in her head whenever she doubts herself in life, or on set.

"SCAVENGER" (S6, E4; 2004)

Written By: Dawn DeNoon & Lisa Marie Petersen
Directed By: Daniel Sackheim

A baby is found abandoned with a cryptic note indicating the mother has been kidnapped, thrusting Benson and Stabler into a high-stakes race against time opposite mastermind Humphrey Becker, a cunning copycat of the "RDK" (Rape, Dismember, Kill) serial killer who taunts the SVU with a series of riddles and clues, each more twisted than the last.

WHY IT'S ICONIC: This is the first episode of *SVU* to have a suspect use puzzles, clues, and riddles to bait detectives into various smokescreens. This episode unlocked new storytelling potential and incorporated more cat-and-mouse elements as opposed to a traditional investigation.

CASE FILES: The "RDK" murderer is based on the real-life killer Dennis Rader, known as BTK (Bind, Torture, Kill). Becker's note explaining his motives eerily echoes Rader, who once wrote, "How many do I have to kill before I get a name in the paper or some national attention?"

WRAP SHEET: Becker's eccentric mother is played by Anne Meara, half of comedy duo Stiller and Meara with husband Jerry Stiller (parents of actor Ben). She also appears in another *SVU* episode, "Dreams Deferred" (S14, E9; 2012) as the mother of Patricia Arquette.

"CONSCIENCE" (S6, E6; 2004)

Written By: Robert Nathan & Roger Wolfson
Directed By: David Platt

Five-year-old Henry Morton vanishes at a birthday party and is later found dead. Suspicion initially falls on a local sex offender, but the true culprit is much closer to home. The case reaches its boiling point in court, where grief, rage, and impossible moral dilemmas collide.

WHY IT'S ICONIC: A chilling study of juvenile sociopathy, this episode asks: Should a child killer be shown leniency or are some people beyond rehabilitation? The ending still shocks fans.

CASE FILES: Guest star Kyle MacLachlan (*Twin Peaks* and *Sex and the City*) plays Dr. Brett Morton, the grieving father of the victim. This served as a reunion for MacLachlan and Dann Florek, who previously appeared in 1994's *The Flintstones* together as Cliff Vandercave and Mr. Slate, respectively.

WRAP SHEET: Dr. Morton's defense lawyer, Chauncey Zeirko (a recurring defense attorney), is played by Peter Riegert, who made his acting debut in 1978 as Donald "Boon" Schoenstein in *National Lampoon's Animal House*.

"CHARISMA" (S6, E7; 2004)

Written By: Tara Butters & Michele Fazekas
Directed By: Arthur W. Forney

When twelve-year-old Melanie Cramer is admitted to the hospital pregnant, all eyes are on Abraham, the leader of the "Church of Wisdom and Sight," a dangerous cult rife with abuse, fraud, and mass brainwashing.

WHY IT'S ICONIC: Holliston Coleman's vulnerable performance as Melanie and Jeff Kober's creepy-yet-charismatic Abraham take the story to new heights. Benson's explosive confrontation with Melanie's mother is a rare but powerful moment of Benson unleashing the rage we all were feeling.

CASE FILES: This episode is loosely based on the case of Marcus Wesson (the "vampire king of Fresno"), who terrified the nation by leading an incestuous cult and fathering children with his daughters and nieces.

WRAP SHEET: This wasn't the first time Jeff Kober and Ice-T worked together—they both starred in the 1994 feature film adaptation of the comic book *Tank Girl*.

"IDENTITY" (S6, E12; 2005)

Written By: Lisa Marie Petersen & Dawn DeNoon
Directed By: Rick Wallace

The murder of a gang member leads Benson and Stabler to twins Logan and Lindsay, whose lives have been shaped by a very dark secret. Lindsay, raised as female after a botched circumcision, learns that she was born male, which shatters her sense of self. Their manipulative therapist, Dr. Blair, treats them like test subjects during years of abuse. As the investigation escalates, one of the twins takes justice into their own hands.

WHY IT'S ICONIC: Tackling medical ethics, abuse, and gender identity long before it was mainstream, "Identity" explores nature versus nurture, and features a gut-wrenching performance by Reiley McClendon.

CASE FILES: This episode is loosely based on the true story of David Reimer, a Canadian man whose gender was reassigned after a botched circumcision.

WRAP SHEET: The unforgettable performances of twins Logan and Lindsay are all thanks to one actor, Reiley McClendon, who took on both roles. Thanks to clever editing, body doubles, and visual effects, both of McClendon's performances could be seen simultaneously.

"911" (S7, E3; 2005)

Written By: Patrick Harbinson
Directed By: Ted Kotcheff

A rare night off for Benson is interrupted by a desperate 911 call from Maria, a frightened nine-year-old claiming she's been trapped for days. As the team races to trace the manipulated signal, doubts grow about the call's authenticity—but Benson remains convinced Maria is in danger.

WHY IT'S ICONIC: This Stabler-free episode puts all the emotional and investigative weight on Benson's shoulders, earning Hargitay her first (and only) Emmy win. It's also the highest-rated *SVU* episode on IMDb, with a rating of 9.3 out of 10. Nearly twenty years later, Maria returns in "Probability of Doom" (S25, E7; 2024), now a police academy graduate following in Benson's footsteps—until she's tragically killed in *Law & Order*'s "Play With Fire Part 1" (S24, E19; 2025), prompting a crossover event where Benson assists the Twenty-Seventh Precinct.

CASE FILES: Hargitay filmed all her phone scenes opposite a script supervisor reading Maria's lines with no emotion. She definitely earned that Emmy!

WRAP SHEET: Before he was an Executive Producer on *SVU*, Ted Kotcheff was primarily known for directing feature films like the Australian cult classic *Wake in Fright* and Sylvester Stallone's first Rambo film, *First Blood*.

"RAW" (S7, E6; 2005)

Written By: Dawn DeNoon
Directed By: Jonathan Kaplan

A school shooting leaves one child dead and two others injured. While tracking leads, the SVU uncovers an unrelated child abuse case before Munch traces a gun to a Staten Island gun shop revealed to be a front for "RAW" (Revolution Aryan Warriors), a violent neo-Nazi group.

WHY IT'S ICONIC: *SVU* tackles white supremacy, hate crimes, and domestic terrorism head on. The brutal storytelling, layered narratives, and shocking ending make this a fan favorite.

CASE FILES: In a tender moment, Fin smuggles Munch's favorite fig milkshake (from McGinty's) into the hospital after he's shot in the butt. Sadly, McGinty's isn't real—so you'll have to find your own recipe.

WRAP SHEET: Marcia Gay Harden brings depth and intensity to her role here as FBI agent Dana Lewis, one of *SVU*'s most compelling allies and a fan-favorite character.

"FAULT" (S7, E19; 2006)

Written By: Michele Fazekas & Tara Butters
Directed By: Paul McCrane

When a recently released sex offender murders a family and kidnaps two children, the investigation pushes Benson and Stabler to their limits. Their ironclad partnership—and their personal connection—is tested like never before.

WHY IT'S ICONIC: Bensler fans get a sobering reality check as the characters' closeness finally compromises their judgment. The raw performances from Hargitay, Meloni, and Lou Diamond Phillips make this one of the show's most tension-filled episodes.

CASE FILES: Meloni cites Stabler's "take the shot" moment in this episode as his favorite scene he's done with Hargitay, saying, "We were bound to each other in that moment as people and characters."

WRAP SHEET: This episode was directed by *ER* alum actor Paul McCrane (Dr. Robert Romano). His former *ER* costar Eriq La Salle (Dr. Peter Benton) directed "Burned" (S8, E11; 2007).

"ALTERNATE" (S9, E1; 2007)

Written By: Neal Baer & Dawn DeNoon
Directed By: David Platt

This memorable Season 9 premiere throws Benson and Stabler into a psychological maze as they investigate Janis Donovan, a woman with dissociative identity disorder (DID), whose multiple personalities complicate the case with each new identity being more volatile than the last.

WHY IT'S ICONIC: Cynthia Nixon's Emmy-winning performance effortlessly shifts between distinct personalities and keeps viewers on edge. While some found Nixon's portrayal over-the-top (even Stabler seemed ready for a Christopher Walken impression), others call it just right—showcasing *SVU*'s knack for morally complex narratives.

CASE FILES: Authenticity doesn't come cheap! Remember the scene with Janis huddled inside a cave at Innwood Hill Park? Since there are no actual caves in Manhattan, the production team built one from scratch in a nearby warehouse, using Styrofoam to mimic natural rock formations. The price tag? $50,000—a small price to pay to create a believable setting without leaving the city.

WRAP SHEET: Adding to the episode's impact, guest star Bronson Pinchot (*Beverly Hills Cop, Perfect Strangers*) played Janis's psychiatrist and praised the welcoming environment on set, calling Hargitay and Meloni "the most welcoming stars of any show I've ever guested on."

"PATERNITY" (S9, E9; 2007)

Written By: Amanda Green
Directed By: Kate Woods

A bloodied little boy is found wandering the streets, leading the SVU to a murdered nanny and a tangled web of family betrayal. Meanwhile, Stabler faces a personal crisis: his wife Kathy is pregnant, and doubts about the baby's paternity arise.

WHY IT'S ICONIC: This episode shifts the procedural drama to the B story, instead focusing on Stabler's family turmoil. The tension peaks with Benson saving Kathy and her unborn child. While some question the plausibility of Benson inserting an IV correctly, the raw emotion and life-or-death stakes make it unforgettable.

CASE FILES: This episode marks the first-ever on-screen hug between Benson and Stabler. Hargitay reflected, "Chris surprised me with it, and it was so right. You can feel everything unspoken, almost more than the spoken word."

WRAP SHEET: "Paternity" highlights *SVU*'s love for the name Tommy. Viewers have clocked over thirty characters with this name, a fact once addressed by showrunner Warren Leight. He explained that names like Tommy are chosen because they're common enough to avoid legal conflicts and misunderstandings, making them go-to picks for recurring characters.

"UNDERCOVER" (S9, E15; 2008)

Written By: Mark Goffman
Directed By: David Platt

When a teenage girl is found raped in a community garden, the case leads Benson and Stabler to her mother, an inmate at a women's prison. Digging deeper, they uncover a chilling web of abuse and corruption, inspiring Benson to go undercover and risk her safety in a brutal environment.

WHY IT'S ICONIC: Hargitay's fearless performance earned her a fifth Emmy nomination, particularly for two unforgettable moments: Benson's stark admission to Warner after being asked if she was raped and her quiet reflection after Stabler inquired about the basement. Johnny Messner's terrifying portrayal of Lowell Harris makes this an all-time classic.

CASE FILES: This is the first time Ice-T appears without his signature ponytail, adding an additional layer of intrigue for fans.

WRAP SHEET: Hargitay described this as one of the most emotionally and physically taxing experiences of her career, noting, "I threw up afterward. I wanted to go as far as I could to make it as real and frightening as it is for people who are assaulted." The episode's inclusion of Benson's near-assault sparked important conversations about vulnerability and resilience, as Hargitay added, "That was a really important message to send—that sexual assault doesn't discriminate."

"AUTHORITY" (S9, E17; 2008)

Written By: Neal Baer & Amanda Green
Directed By: David Platt

When an employee at a fast-food restaurant files a complaint about a degrading strip search conducted by her manager, the squad uncovers a disturbing web of hoax calls orchestrated by Merritt Rook, a brilliant but unhinged audio engineer waging a personal campaign against authority.

WHY IT'S ICONIC: How could an *SVU* episode featuring the late great Robin Williams *not* be iconic? In his chilling and charismatic performance as Merritt Rook, Williams brings to life one of the show's most complex villains in an episode that delves into themes of blind obedience, power dynamics, and the human capacity to question authority.

CASE FILES: This milestone two hundredth episode of the series was inspired by Improv Everywhere's viral "Frozen Grand Central" stunt, the 2004 resolution of the Mount Washington strip search scam, and the infamous Milgram obedience experiments—Rook's pseudonym is even "Milgram."

WRAP SHEET: On set, Williams charmed everyone, including Mariska Hargitay's toddler, with his iconic humor and funny voices. Cast and crew still remember this episode as one of their favorites to film.

"WILDLIFE" (S10, E7; 2008)

Written By: Mick Betancourt
Directed By: Peter Leto

After the strange circumstances of a young model's death—mauled by a tiger and found with an exotic bird in her purse—lead to shocking connections to murder and illegal trading, Stabler goes undercover as a crooked customs agent to infiltrate a Russian animal smuggling ring as the team supports him from afar. The mission tests his limits, his marriage, and his safety.

WHY IT'S ICONIC: This episode has *everything*. Exotic animals, edge-of-your-seat drama, death by tiger, irradiated turtle eggs, Outkast's Big Boi getting eaten by hyenas, and a steamy improvised moment for Bensler fans.

CASE FILES: During a rooftop chase at the end of the episode, Mariska Hargitay suffered a serious injury. At first, she thought she'd just had the wind knocked out of her and ignored the injury until three months later, when the pain started getting worse. An X-ray revealed that her right lung was 50 percent collapsed, requiring surgery and time off.

WRAP SHEET: Dann Florek revealed on an episode of *That's Messed Up: An SVU Podcast* that a fan gifted him a painting of Cragen holding Kimba, the gibbon he rescued from a basketball in this episode. He still cherishes the painting as one of his favorite fan tributes.

"BALLERINA" (S10, E16; 2009)

Written By: Daniel Truly
Directed By: Peter Leto

When bodies are discovered in an apparent murder–suicide, the investigation leads the SVU to Birdie Sulloway, the glamorous yet sinister building owner (played by the legendary Carol Burnett). Birdie, a former dancer, harbors dark secrets and flaunts her twisted, codependent relationship with her much younger "nephew"-turned-lover, Chet.

WHY IT'S ICONIC: "Ballerina" delivers because of its unlikely duo: Carol Burnett and Matthew Lillard. One standout moment features Burnett channeling *Sunset Boulevard* as she watches real-life footage of herself, waxing poetic about the past.

CASE FILES: Carol Burnett received an Emmy nomination for her performance but lost to Ellen Burstyn, who guest-starred as Stabler's mother in "Swing" (S10, E3; 2008).

WRAP SHEET: Working on *SVU* reminded Burnett of the tight-knit bond and professionalism of her own legendary show, *The Carol Burnett Show*. Burnett said, "It's a well-oiled machine . . . It reminds me of our crew because we were on for eleven years and we were family." She also relished stepping into such a sinister role, sharing, "I loved that I wasn't playing for laughs."

"ZEBRAS" (S10, E22; 2009)

Written By: Amanda Green & Daniel Truly
Directed By: Peter Leto

A father and daughter rollerblading through Central Park discover a woman's body. The SVU quickly identifies a suspect, but when bumbling forensic tech Dale Stuckey makes a filing error, their suspect is released, and another murder follows. The wild climax? A rogue kiss, a sushi order, and Benson saving Stabler with a perfectly placed kick.

WHY IT'S ICONIC: Few episodes balance dark humor, tension, and shocking reveals quite like this one. Plus, we get to see Munch's ex-wife, portrayed by Carol Kane (*Scrooged, Annie Hall, The Princess Bride*), who adds even more texture to Richard Belzer's already layered performance.

CASE FILES: The title refers to the medical saying, "When you hear hoofbeats, think horses, not zebras," reminding us that sometimes the obvious answer is the right one. This episode also marks the first and only time *SVU* has killed off a recurring forensics character.

WRAP SHEET: Kane and Belzer previously shared screen time as Gwen Munch and Detective John Munch back in 1997 on *Homicide: Life on the Street*, where Detective Munch originated.

"SHADOW" S11, E12 (2010)

Written By: Amanda Green
Directed By: Amy Redford

A wealthy couple is found dead in what appears to be a murder–suicide, but the case takes a turn when the victims' daughter, Anne Gillette, claims she is being stalked—and the so-called stalker is actually Detective Ashok Ramsey from Special Frauds, investigating Anne for embezzlement.

WHY IT'S ICONIC: "Shadow" is camp at its best—a masterclass in psychological drama and sinister villainy. Plus, Fin goes undercover, which is always a treat. *Plus*, we get a juicy performance by Emmy-, Tony-, and Golden Globe-winning actress Sarah Paulson. Need we say more?

CASE FILES: When teenage pictures of Anne are shown to the SVU, they are actually pictures of Sarah Paulson's Season 5 appearance on The Mothership.

WRAP SHEET: The director of this episode (which is based on the infamous Lizzie Borden case) is Amy Redford, the daughter of Hollywood legend Robert Redford.

"BEHAVE" (S12, E3; 2010)

Written By: Jonathan Greene
Directed By: Helen Shaver

When a woman is found battered and claims she's been raped, again, Benson and Stabler uncover a horrifying truth—she's been assaulted by the same man for fifteen years. Their investigation leads to a predator who has stalked, assaulted, and terrorized women across the country. But with the statute of limitations closing on any chance for justice, Benson takes matters into her own hands, exposing the nationwide backlog of untested rape kits that have allowed this predator to remain free for decades.

WHY IT'S ICONIC: Take a searing indictment of the nationwide backlog of untested rape kits, add Hollywood star Jennifer Love Hewitt (with an emotionally devastating performance), and let Benson travel outside of NYC to multiple cities to find the truth, and you have one action-packed episode with a thrilling ending that has stood the test of time.

CASE FILES: This episode was inspired by the real-life story of Helena Lazaro, a survivor whose rape kit remained untested for years. Showrunner Neal Baer was moved to write the story after he attended an event hosted by Mariska Hargitay for her Joyful Heart Foundation where he heard real survivors' stories.

WRAP SHEET: The episode was a backdoor pilot for *Law & Order: Los Angeles* (2010), which starred Skeet Ulrich (*Scream*) as Detective Rex Winters. It became the third *Law & Order* series to be canceled by NBC and the second to be canceled after only one season (after *Law & Order: Trial by Jury*).

"DREAMS DEFERRED" (S14, E9; 2012)

Written By: Julie Martin & Warren Leight
Directed By: Michael Smith

The SVU teams up with the FBI in a high-stakes manhunt for Craig Rasmussen, a spree killer leaving a trail of bodies across New York City. Their best chance at catching him? Jeannie Kerns, a sex worker with a crucial connection to the suspect and a troubled past of her own.

WHY IT'S ICONIC: Patricia Arquette's memorable performance anchors this emotional powerhouse of an episode. Fans and critics have praised the striking cold open montage, which intercuts Jeannie preparing for work with Craig Rasmussen embarking on his killing spree. Set to the haunting tune of James Blunt's "I'll Take Everything," the sequence crescendos with the last line of the chorus leaving viewers unsettled and captivated.

CASE FILES: Showrunner Warren Leight explained that the episode contributed to the season's intentional thematic exploration of "secrets" and deeper dives into the lives of those they serve.

WRAP SHEET: Actor P.J. Brown's portrayal of killer Craig Rasmussen was his fifth and last appearance on an *SVU* episode. Fittingly, his first episode was also the show's first, "Payback" (S1, E1; 1999), where he played Frank Bremmer, a Crime Scene Unit officer who briefs Stabler and Benson when they arrive at the rainy crime scene. Brown uttered the first words ever spoken on the series.

"BORN PSYCHOPATH" (S14, E19; 2013)

"POST-GRADUATE PSYCHOPATH"

(S22, E14; 2021)

Written By: Julie Martin & Warren Leight ("Born Psychopath"); Brianna Yellen & Micharne Cloughley ("Post-Graduate Psychopath")

Directed By: Alex Chapple ("Born Psychopath"); Norberto Barba ("Post-Graduate Psychopath")

In "Born Psychopath," the squad investigates a young girl named Ruby who is covered in bruises. The trail leads them to Henry, her ten-year-old brother whose behavior (violence, manipulation, attempted murder) forces everyone to face an unnerving truth: Henry is a child psychopath. Nearly a decade later in "Post-Graduate Psychopath," Henry, now eighteen, is free to rejoin society, but continues his reign of terror and leaves the SVU in shambles as they try to stop him once again.

WHY THEY'RE ICONIC: These episodes form one of *SVU*'s most disturbing sagas. "Born Psychopath" introduced Henry as a chilling figure, embodying the nature versus nurture debate in terrifying ways. "Post-Graduate Psychopath" raises the stakes by reintroducing him as a young adult who's only grown more dangerous.

CASE FILES: Actor Ethan Cutkosky (*Shameless*) earned rave reviews from fans and critics alike for his near-decade apart portrayals of Henry. Kelli Giddish gives perhaps the biggest stamp of approval to his performance, as she's admitted both these episodes have always haunted her.

WRAP SHEET: Fans of *Stranger Things* might be surprised to spot Caleb McLaughlin (Lucas) in "Born Psychopath" as a young student in the classroom scene—his television acting debut.

"SURRENDER BENSON" (S15, E1; 2013)

Written By: Julie Martin & Warren Leight
Directed By: Michael Smith

In perhaps Benson's darkest hour, this harrowing season premiere finds her held captive and fighting for her life at the hands of sadistic serial rapist and murderer William Lewis.

WHY IT'S ICONIC: A masterclass in tension, "Surrender Benson" allows Hargitay to deliver one of her most gut-wrenching performances and proved that, even after fifteen seasons (and nearly fifteen years), she could still bring the heat. It also demonstrated the power of the *SVU* fan community: following the intense cliffhanger of "Her Negotiation" (S14, E24; 2013), where Benson is abducted by William Lewis, worried fans launched the viral #SaveBenson campaign to express concern and build anticipation for this Season 15 premiere. NBC embraced the movement, engaged with viewers, and amplified the buzz, and it contributed to "Surrender Benson" becoming one of *SVU*'s most-watched premieres.

CASE FILES: Showrunner Warren Leight set out to create the most evil *SVU* villain, and William Lewis delivered. Pablo Schreiber's performance earned widespread acclaim. The episode also introduced Benson's therapist, Dr. Peter Lindstrom (Bill Irwin), a key figure in her healing.

WRAP SHEET: Hargitay described this episode as one of the most challenging of her career, saying, "It was painful to film, but it was also an important story to tell."

HONORABLE MENTIONS

INFLUENTIAL IN THEIR OWN WAYS, THESE HONORABLE MENTIONS SHOULD ALWAYS BE INCLUDED IN THE CONVERSATION, EVEN IF WE COULDN'T SQUEEZE THEM INTO OUR LIST OF ESSENTIAL EPISODES.

"CLOSURE"
(S1, E10; 2000) &
"CLOSURE: PART 2"
(S2, E3; 2000)

The first time the show utilizes a returning victim and creates a sequel-like format, diving deep into the psyche of an assault victim in a way that many shows wouldn't touch.

"NOCTURNE"
(S1, E21; 2000)
& "COMPETENCE"
(S3, E22; 2002)

These two heartbreaking episodes, airing early in the show's run, put a spotlight on under-discussed issues such as the vicious cycle of abuse among men ("Nocturne") and people with developmental disabilities being victims of sexual assault ("Competence").

"VENOM" (S7, E18; 2006) &
"SCREWED" (S8, E22; 2007)

These two gripping episodes featuring guest star Chris "Ludacris" Bridges prove that while most guest stars are good, when you have a *great* guest star, it makes you want to "Stand Up."

"DAYDREAM BELIEVER"
(S16, E20; 2015)

Dick Wolf is a master of getting us to clear our schedules on any given night . . . *especially* when there's an epic crossover with his other properties, like this one which merges *SVU* and *Chicago P.D.*

"SURRENDERING NOAH"
(S16, E23; 2015)

Benson deserves happiness just like everyone else, and she finally gets a taste of it when she officially adopts her son, Noah. Of course, there has to be a hefty side of murder and tension.

"GAMBLER'S FALLACY" (S15, E17; 2014)

Teleplay By: Julie Martin & Warren Leight
Story By: Kevin Fox
Directed By: Alex Chapple

Detective Amanda Rollins spirals out of control when her gambling addiction leads her to an illegal club where she is recognized as a cop. To protect her career, she strikes a deal that pulls her into a web of criminal favors, culminating in stolen evidence and a harsh reckoning.

WHY IT'S ICONIC: A rare character-driven episode focusing on Rollins's personal struggles. This episode also introduces Declan O'Rourke (Donal Logue), whose dual role as criminal club manager and undercover cop kept viewers guessing.

CASE FILES: The title refers to the cognitive bias whereby people falsely believe past events will affect future outcomes, which was made famous by the 1913 Monte Carlo roulette incident where the ball landed on black twenty-six times in a row, prompting gamblers to bet heavily on red, assuming it was due.

WRAP SHEET: Upon reading the script, Kelli Giddish recalled, "I jumped up and down in my dressing room!" She's called it one of her most challenging episodes and added, "I love toeing that line . . . I'd much rather play somebody that's got secrets than someone that's safe."

"HEARTFELT PASSAGES" (S17, E23; 2016)

Written By: Warren Leight & Julie Martin
Directed By: Alex Chapple

SVU's Season 17 finale delivers a gut-wrenching story centered on a corrupt corrections officer, Gary Munson, who faces multiple rape charges. When Munson's wife attempts to flee with their children, Sergeant Mike Dodds steps in to help—but his selfless act leads to tragic consequences.

WHY IT'S ICONIC: From Barba's pursuit of justice to Dodds's ultimate sacrifice, "Heartfelt Passages" raises the stakes like few episodes have. Ed Tucker also says Benson's full name—Olivia *Margaret* Benson—for the first time in the show's history.

CASE FILES: This episode marked the shocking end of Andy Karl's tenure, with Dodds becoming the first member of the squad to die in the line of duty. Karl described his farewell as "an emotional goodbye to a family I'll always cherish."

WRAP SHEET: Behind the scenes, actor Andy Karl left *SVU* after his one-season arc to become Phil Connors in the West End and then Broadway musical adaptation of the Bill Murray classic, *Groundhog Day*. Yet another example of *SVU*'s commitment to highlighting theater actors.

CURATED BY BENSON

Ahead of the Season 22 premiere, streaming platform Peacock asked Mariska Hargitay to curate a list of ten episodes for fans to watch to gear up for the new premiere. Here are the titles she chose. Would you have curated the same list?

"Loss" (S5, E4; 2003)

"Identity" (S6, E12;2005)

"911" (S7, E3; 2005)

"Fault" (S7, E19; 2006)

"Paternity" (S9, E9; 2007)

"Undercover" (S9, E15; 2008)

"Wildlife" (S10, E7; 2008)

"Born Psychopath" (S14, E19; 2013)

"Surrender Benson" (S15, E1; 2013)

"Return of the Prodigal Son"
(S22, E9; 2021)

"CORNERED" (S26, E8; 2024)

Written By: David Graziano & Julie Martin
Directed By: Juan José Campanella

Carisi stops at his favorite deli to buy flowers for his paralegal's birthday but unknowingly walks into a violent hostage situation. With Benson coordinating outside and Rollins racing to the scene, the squad fights to save Carisi before it's too late.

WHY IT'S ICONIC: Newer episodes of a long-running series rarely enter "Best Of" lists, but *Cornered* proves that after twenty-five-plus years, *SVU* can still deliver the high-stakes storytelling fans expect. Scanavino shines in a career-highlight performance and the episode reinforces *SVU*'s message: crime is unpredictable, and no one—not even the good guys—are safe.

CASE FILES: Scanavino revealed that the hardest scene to film was Carisi refusing to let Benson exchange herself as a hostage: "I kind of have to make this decision that this is my responsibility and that I can't just let my friend walk into peril when I was the unfortunate one to walk into the deli in the first place."

WRAP SHEET: Before joining the main cast as Carisi, Scanavino played Johnny Dubcek, a janitor who takes the law into his own hands in "Monster's Legacy" (S14, E13; 2013), an episode also featuring boxing legend Mike Tyson, which left some fans scratching their heads due to Tyson's own past legal troubles.

TOP 5 LISTS

Every die-hard fan has their own collection of Top 5 lists ready to bust out at parties or among like-minded friends. To get you started in your conversations and debates, here are just a handful of themed rankings.

BENSLER MOMENTS

Honorable Mention: When Benson and Stabler admitted they'd trade kidneys with each other.

"Choreographed" (S8, E9; 2006)

5. The almost-kiss in Benson's kitchen. *Stop teasing us already!* **"Blood Out"** (S24, E12; 2023)
4. Arguably the look that started it all—outside the squad car after Stabler compares Benson to a monk. **"A Single Life"** (S1, E2; 1999)
3. When Stabler drives all the way uptown from the Queensboro Bridge, drops off the car, picks up the sedan, turns around, and drives all the way back downtown for Benson. And then they share orange juice. **"Stalked"** (S1, E8; 1999)
2. Stabler chooses Benson's life over a child hostage. **"Fault"** (S7, E19; 2006) *
1. The hug. Enough said. **"Paternity"** (S9, E9; 2007)

* Hargitay was actually eight months pregnant with her son August during filming, which added another layer of complexity to the already high-stakes episode.

TWIST ENDINGS

Honorable Mention: "Bedtime" (S11, E18; 2010)

5. **"Bombshell"** (S12, E19; 2011)
4. **"Damaged"** (S4, E11; 2003) *
3. **"Collateral Damages"** (S17, E15; 2016)
2. **"Zebras"** (S10, E22; 2009)
1. **"Send in the Clowns"** (S19, E17; 2018)

* Inspired by the killing spree of Paul Bernardo and Karla Homolka, who were known as the Ken and Barbie Killers.

UNDERCOVER MOMENTS

Honorable Mention: Benson tells off a creep in Russian while undercover at a meat packing plant.

"Beef" (S11, E20; 2010) *

5. Carisi goes undercover at a homeless shelter and trades his signature cannoli for donut holes. **"Sheltered Outcasts"** (S17, E19; 2016)
4. The squad goes undercover at a rave. Benson and Jeffries put in effort while the guys look like three dads at a prom. Stabler's idea of undercover? Unbuttoning his shirt. **"Runaway"** (S2, E16; 2001)
3. Stabler and Benson go undercover as swingers. **"Bombshell"** (S12, E19; 2011)
2. Munch goes undercover as a homeless conspiracy theorist screaming in the street. We know—practically unrecognizable. **"Babes"** (S10, E6; 2008)

1. Benson thinks quickly and saves Stabler's undercover mission by posing as a sex worker in a shirtless Bensler scene that *still* has fans talking.
"Wildlife" (S10, E7; 2008)

* Mariska Hargitay can speak five languages: English, French, Hungarian, Spanish, and Italian.

COURTROOM SCENES

Honorable Mention: "Heightened Emotions" (S18, E4; 2016)

5. **"The Long Arm of the Witness"** (S22, E6; 2021)
4. **"Institutional Fail"** (S17, E4; 2015)
3. **"Twenty-Five Acts"** (S14, E3; 2012)
2. **"Doubt"** (S6, E8; 2004) *
1. **"Raw"** (S7, E6; 2005)

* This episode is famous for its unusually ambiguous ending that left viewers to decide whether Ron Polikoff (played by Billy Campbell) was guilty or innocent in a classic "he said, she said" case.

UNDERRATED EPISODES

Honorable Mention: "Control" (S5, E9; 2003)*

5. **"Bedtime"** (S11, E18; 2010)
4. **"Guilt"** (S3, E18; 2002)
3. **"Selfish"** (S10, E19; 2009)
2. **"Coerced"** (S5, E6; 2003)
1. **"Manhunt"** (S2, E18; 2001)

* This episode features a cameo from Mickey Hargitay, father of Mariska Hargitay, playing "Grandfather," the man who describes the escalator incident to Benson in the teaser.

HEARTBREAKING DEATHS

Honorable Mention: Ed Tucker (Robert John Burke)

5. **Kathy Stabler** (Isabel Gillies)
4. **Sonya Paxton** (Christine Lahti)
3. **Mike Dodds** (Andy Karl)
2. **Sister Peg** (Charlayne Woodard) *
1. **Ryan O'Halloran** (Mike Doyle) *

* Fans often have healthy disagreements about characters, episodes, plotlines or which era of *SVU* is best, but one thing most fans agree upon is that these two characters, along with Dana Lewis, were done dirty by the writing staff. Shame!

ADAs

Honorable Mention: Abbie Carmichael (Angie Harmon) *

5. **Dominick Carisi, Jr.** (Peter Scanavino)
4. **Peter Stone** (Philip Winchester)
3. **Rafael Barba** (Raúl Esparza)
2. **Casey Novak** (Diane Neal)
1. **Alexandra Cabot** (Stephanie March) *

* Future ADA actresses Angie Harmon and Stephanie March attended the same high school (Highland Park High in Dallas, TX), at the same time, and had the same computer class, but never knew each other!

DEFENSE ATTORNEYS

Honorable Mentions: Carolyn Maddox (CCH Pounder) and (if only because we love to hate him) **John Buchanan** (Delaney Williams)

5. **Roger Kressler** (Ned Eisenberg)
4. **Trevor Langan** (Peter Hermann) *
3. **Donna Emmett** (Viola Davis)
2. **Rita Calhoun** (Elizabeth Marvel)
1. **Bayard Ellis** (Andre Braugher)

* Langan is the longest-running defense attorney in show history. Actor Peter Hermann met his future wife (Mariska Hargitay) during his first appearance in "Monogamy" (S3, E11; 2002). Their first date? A church service where Mariska had a lightning-bolt moment and knew he was "the one." They tied the knot in 2004, and have since built a loving family with three kids.

MOST TERRIFYING VILLAINS

Honorable Mention: Marilyn Nesbit (Diane Venora)

5. **Dr. Carl Rudnick** (Jefferson Mays)
4. **Lowell Harris** (Johnny Messner)
3. **Victor Paul Gitano** (Lou Diamond Phillips)
2. **Dr. Greg Yates** (Dallas Roberts)
1. **William Lewis** (Pablo Schreiber) *

* Mariska Hargitay revealed to *Today* that "Surrender Benson," alongside Pablo Schreiber's William Lewis, was the most difficult episode she had ever shot. "I have to tell you, after fifteen years, to be nervous and scared and excited to go to work—it's a pretty great thing."

THE PRIME SUSPECTS

RITE OF PASSAGE

It's hard to watch *SVU* without IMDb open because you're often wondering, "Wait, where have I seen that actor before?" Credit goes to the stellar casting department, whose well-chosen guest stars can bring levity to dark themes. If *SVU*'s main cast is the starting lineup, its guest stars are the sixth man, coming off the bench to light up the scoreboard. Whether it's a future A-lister or beloved actor chewing up the scenery, the guest stars rarely miss. Will any of these stars make a return on *SVU*? Never say never. Unless you've been waiting for Benson and Stabler to kiss . . . in that case, you're waiting *at least* twenty-five-to-life!

FROM UNKNOWN TO UNDER OATH: BEFORE THEY WERE FAMOUS

SVU has two undeniable superpowers: crafting gripping, can't-look-away stories and turning unknown actors into future stars. With over five hundred episodes, the show's get rate is impressive. *SVU* is where fresh talent gets thrown into the deep end and comes out the other end an even better actor than before. Lee Pace was far from *Pushing Daisies* when he played a victim of assault in his first-ever role in "Guilt" (S3, E18; 2002), actress/director Elizabeth Banks was *Pitch Perfect* as a vengeful backstabbing mother in "Sacrifice" (S3, E7; 2001), and David Harbour was into much *Stranger Things* in his second-ever role as a doll-obsessed pedophile in "Dolls" (S4, E7; 2002). Let's explore some other iconic *SVU* origin stories.

SARAH HYLAND

Before charming audiences as Haley Dunphy (*Modern Family*) and in other roles on stage and screen, Hyland turned in two powerhouse performances on *SVU*.

"Repression" (S3, E1; 2001)

Role: Lily, the seven-year-old sister to Megan, a college student manipulated by her psychiatrist into believing she was molested.

"Hothouse" (S10, E12; 2009)

Role: Deeply troubled and highly competitive student Jennifer Banks, who is central to the case of a murdered child prodigy and—spoiler—gives one of the show's greatest confessions.

Did you know? Airing just two weeks after 9/11, "Repression" is the only *SVU* episode to feature a modified opening monologue in tribute to the victims and first responders.

ADAM DRIVER

Driver, a former Marine, showcased versatility in smaller roles before hitting it big in *Girls*, *Marriage Story*, and as Kylo Ren in the *Star Wars* sequel trilogy.

"Theatre Tricks" (S13, E11; 2012)

Role: Jason Roberts, a socially awkward techie-turned-suspect obsessed with an actress who is assaulted during an interactive theater production.

Did you know? This episode's cast includes comedian Gilbert Gottfried, actor/director Fisher Stevens (*Short Circuit, Hackers*), actor Kevin Pollak (*A Few Good Men, The Marvelous Mrs. Maisel*), and Coco Austin, Ice-T's wife, in her third *SVU* appearance.

SABRINA CARPENTER

Before she was a Disney star (*Girl Meets World*) and the Grammy-winning singer of "Espresso," Carpenter made her on-screen acting debut on *SVU* at just eleven years old.

"Possessed" (S12, E12; 2011)

Role: Paula Moretti, a brave young girl who opens up to Stabler about Coventry, a child exploitation network, despite threats to her and her father's safety.

Did you know? During this episode you can clearly see a photo on Benson's desk of her with former President Barack Obama at an event. This is a real photo of Hargitay and Obama with Barbara Walters (cropped out) standing beside her.

Look for the real-life snapshot of Hargitay's mother, actress Jayne Mansfield, often featured on Benson's desk—it's the one of a woman grocery shopping while carrying two tiny dogs and wearing a pointed hat. A touching tribute to her mother's life and career.

A VERY PRESIDENTIAL CAMEO

In 2016, then-Vice President (and future President) Joe Biden guest-starred as himself in "Making a Rapist" (S18, E2; 2016), praising Benson for tackling the backlog of untested rape kits. This cameo highlighted Biden's real-life work on the Violence Against Women Act and advocacy for sexual assault survivors.

IAN SOMERHALDER

Before captivating audiences as Boone Carlyle, a survivor of Oceanic Flight 815 on *Lost*, and as the malevolent vampire Damon Salvatore on *The Vampire Diaries*, Somerhalder turned up the heat in this early role.

"Dominance" (S4, E20; 2003)

Role: Charlie Baker, a manipulative sociopath who coerces his brother into a brutal killing spree.

Did you know? This episode also features Jason Ritter as Billy, and Oscar nominee Frank Langella as their father, Al. The brutal events of this episode are inspired by the equally brutal events of the "Wichita Massacre," a 2000 killing spree in Kansas.

KATE MARA & ROONEY MARA

KATE MARA

Before *House of Cards, Brokeback Mountain,* and *The Martian,* Kate's first acting gig was a guest role on the original *Law & Order*, which launched her career.

"Pixies" (S2, E9; 2001)

Role: Lori, a competitive gymnast whose jealousy and resentment drive her to confront a teammate standing in the way of her ambitions.

ROONEY MARA

Known for *The Social Network* and her Oscar-nominated roles in *The Girl with the Dragon Tattoo* and *Carol*, Rooney made her TV debut on *SVU*.

"Fat" (S7, E20; 2006)

Role: Jessica DeLay, a teenage assault victim who bullies overweight individuals—including her attackers and their disabled brother—due to her own past trauma.

Did you know? The sisters hail from football royalty—their mother's family (the Rooneys) founded the Pittsburgh Steelers in 1933 and their father's family (the Maras) founded the New York Giants in 1925.

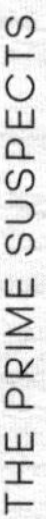

FROM ARENAS TO SUBPOENAS: MUSICIANS MEET MUNCH

Whether they're playing heroes, victims, suspects, or snitches, *SVU* provides a safe space for musicians to flex their acting chops, with Ice-T, one of their own, already in the cast. From Jesse McCartney losing his "Beautiful Soul" as a murderous boyfriend in "Babes" (S10, E6; 2008) to watching Wu-Tang's Method Man "Bring the Pain" as a notorious gangster in "Snitch" (S9, E10; 2007) or seeing Heavy D (without his Boyz) show his "Criminal Mind" as a murderous manager in "Personal Fouls" (S13, E2; 2011), *SVU* loves to blend music and justice.

CHRIS "LUDACRIS" BRIDGES

This Grammy-winning rapper with hits like "Yeah!," "Stand Up," and "Southern Hospitality" also plays Tej Parker in *The Fast & The Furious* franchise.

"Venom" (S7, E18; 2006) and **"Screwed"** (S8, E22; 2007)

Role: Darius Parker, a manipulative and disturbed character who exploits the justice system while confronting his estranged family, including Fin.

In "Venom," DNA at a murder scene clears Fin's son, Ken, but reveals a surprising half-brother, Darius, unlocking a complex case for all involved. The culmination of Darius's arc occurs in "Screwed," where he exposes the SVU's secrets in court and, despite his crimes, secures a not-guilty verdict. The episode ends with one of Fin's coldest comebacks.

Did you know? Ludacris also acted in the film *Crash* which, like "Screwed," includes Mark Isham's song "Sense of Touch."

SNOOP DOGG

A legendary rapper and pop culture icon, Snoop Dogg is known for hits like "Gin and Juice" and "Drop It Like It's Hot," his unlikely friendship with Martha Stewart, and his role as a coach on *The Voice*.

"Diss" (S20, E22; 2019)

Role: R.B. Banks, a famous rapper (what else?) entangled in a heated rivalry that spirals into an investigation after his rival's wife is brutally assaulted.

Did you know? Snoop named Ice-T in his top five West Coast rappers of all-time (with E-40, Ice Cube, Too Short, and himself). Ice-T called Snoop, "the most famous and recognizable rapper of all time."

AN INSIDE JOB

Ice-T often fields requests from his friends and collaborators to be on the show. Snoop Dogg called Ice-T and confessed that he hadn't watched *SVU* ever, until he and his wife binged it for twenty-four hours straight and absolutely loved it. A few episodes later, the two hip-hop legends were sharing the screen and fans were ecstatic.

HARRY CONNICK JR.

As a Grammy and Emmy Award–winning jazz artist, musician, talk show host, and actor, Connick has also charmed audiences in *Hope Floats*, *Independence Day*, and *Will & Grace*.

"Official Story" (S13, E12; 2012), **"Father's Shadow"** (S13, E13; 2012), **"Hunting Ground"** (S13, E15; 2012), and **"Justice Denied"** (S13, E17; 2012)

Role: Executive ADA David Haden, a charismatic prosecutor who sparks a rare romance with Benson that they ultimately end to protect the integrity of their work. But the chemistry? Undeniable.

Did you know? Like father, like son . . . sort of! Connick Jr.'s father, Harry Connick Sr., was the District Attorney of Orleans Parish in New Orleans from 1973 to 2003.

AHMIR "QUESTLOVE" THOMPSON

A Grammy-winning musician and Oscar-winning director, Questlove is a cultural icon, music historian, and author who keeps the beat going as the bandleader of The Roots on *The Tonight Show Starring Jimmy Fallon*.

"Criminal Stories" (S15, E18; 2014)

Role: A corpse in the ME's office (uncredited). Questlove revealed in *Us Weekly* that playing a dead body on *Law & Order* was his dream role.

Did you know? This was the first of many *SVU* episodes directed by Mariska Hargitay.

MIRANDA LAMBERT

The Grammy Award–winning country superstar known for "Bluebird" and "Gunpowder & Lead" is also a longtime *SVU* fan and makes her acting debut in the show.

"Father's Shadow" (S13, E13; 2012)

Role: Lacey Ford, a struggling artist caught in a predatory producer's dangerous casting scheme and saved mid-assault by the SVU team.

Did you know? Lambert is the most awarded artist in Academy of Country Music (ACM) history with thirty-seven wins.

DAVE NAVARRO

The guitarist from Jane's Addiction now hosts reality tattoo competition *Ink Master*.

"Funny Valentine" (S14, E16; 2013)

Role: Mr. Ferrari, a loyal sound engineer caught in the middle of a volatile relationship between a rising hip-hop star and his girlfriend which leads to a tragic turn of events.

Did you know? The storyline drew inspiration from the high-profile and tumultuous relationship between musicians Chris Brown and Rihanna.

FROM CHARMING TO CHILLING: PLAYING AGAINST TYPE

If *SVU* has taught us anything, it's that nothing is as it seems—especially for guest stars. Some of the show's most jaw-dropping performances come from actors playing against type, transforming from beloved heroes, sitcom dads, and rom-com leads into villains. In the early days of the show, it was a true shock when Michael Gross (*Family Ties*) turned out to be a killer in "Lust" (S4, E4; 2002), Brat Pack heartthrob Andrew McCarthy went from *Pretty in Pink* to not so pretty in jail in "Slaves" (S1, E22; 2000), or Wonder Woman herself, Lynda Carter, fought on the wrong side of the law in "Design" (S7, E2; 2005) and "Flaw" (*Law & Order* S16, E2; 2005). By later seasons, *SVU* had so perfected this trope that stars behaving off-brand has become almost like a spoiler—but never any less entertaining.

ROBIN WILLIAMS

This Academy Award-winning actor and comedic genius is known for classics like *Mrs. Doubtfire*, *Aladdin*, *Dead Poets Society*, and *Good Will Hunting*.

"Authority" (S9, E17; 2008)

Role: Emmy-nominated turn as Merritt Rook, a sinister audio engineer who impersonates figures of authority to manipulate others into committing horrifying acts.

Did you know? Williams was recruited for *SVU* by longtime friend Richard Belzer after their days doing stand-up.

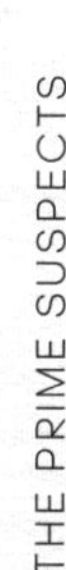

MARTIN SHORT

A Tony and Emmy Award–winning actor and comedian, Martin Short made his mark on *SCTV* and *SNL* before bringing his signature energy to *Three Amigos* and countless collaborations with Steve Martin, including *Only Murders in the Building*.

"Pure" (S6, E18; 2005)

Role: Sebastian Ballentine, a psychotic, self-proclaimed psychic who manipulates his way into an investigation only to be revealed later as Henry Palaver, a predatory virgin rapist.

Did you know? This episode marked a reunion between Martin Short and BD Wong (Dr. George Huang), who previously played partners in the *Father of the Bride* movies.

HENRY WINKLER

This Emmy and Golden Globe Award–winning actor is beloved for his iconic role as Arthur "Fonzie" Fonzarelli on *Happy Days* and his acclaimed turn as Gene Cousineau in *Barry*.

"Greed" (S3, E20; 2002)

Role: Edward Crandall, a con artist posing as devoted husband Edwin Todd while manipulating his way into a woman's life, leading to deception, betrayal, and multiple assaults.

Did you know? Henry Winkler and Richard Belzer are real-life cousins who previously appeared on-screen together in 1982 in the Ron Howard film *Night Shift*.

JERRY LEWIS

A legendary comedian, actor, and filmmaker, Jerry Lewis entertained generations with his slapstick genius in *The Nutty Professor*, his iconic partnership with Dean Martin, and decades of heartfelt hosting on the Labor Day MDA Telethon.

"Uncle" (S8, E4; 2006)

Role: A complex and gripping performance as Detective Munch's mentally ill, homeless uncle Andrew Munch, who becomes entangled in an SVU investigation after befriending a victim.

Did you know? Ice-T admitted he was starstruck, saying, "Jerry Lewis is from the Rat Pack . . . To be with a legend of that caliber—and for him to even know who I was—was big."

HILARY DUFF

An actress, singer, and pop icon, Hilary Duff became a teen idol thanks to *Lizzie McGuire* and chart-topping hits like "So Yesterday," "Wake Up," and "Come Clean," before leading *Younger* and *How I Met Your Father* later in her career.

"Selfish" (S10, E19; 2009)

Role: Ashlee Walker, a self-absorbed and immature young mother whose baby's death sparks an investigation into neglect, lies, family drama, and deeper conversations on personal choice.

Did You Know? Partially inspired by the real-life Casey Anthony case, this darker role marked a major departure for Duff and the episode's subject matter and twists sparked controversy upon airing.

JOHN RITTER

A beloved Emmy Award-winning actor celebrated for his nice guy comedic roles as Jack Tripper in *Three's Company*, Paul Hennessy on *8 Simple Rules*, and his final film appearance in *Bad Santa*.

"Monogamy" (S3, E11; 2002)

Role: Dr. Richard Manning, a jealous psychiatrist driven to a horrific act against his wife and unborn child after discovering her affair with a construction worker played by Bobby Cannavale in an early role.

Did you know? Ritter's son, fellow stage, film, and TV actor Jason Ritter, guest-starred on *SVU* just a year later in "Dominance" (S4, E20; 2003) as victimized murder accomplice Billy Baker, and later took on a different role on The Mothership (S11, E12; 2001).

FROM SITCOMS TO SUSPECTS: WHEN TGIF MEETS *SVU*

Benson and Stabler aren't the only dynamic duo we love to welcome into our homes every week. And when our favorite sitcom stars cross paths with the SVU, there's nothing quite like watching them trade laugh tracks for handcuffs. Without *SVU* we would never have seen Will Arnett (*Arrested Development*) as a human trafficker in "Angels" (S4, E6; 2002), James Van Der Beek (*Dawson's Creek*) as a sexual predator in "Father Dearest" (S13, E20; 2012), or teen idols Melissa Joan Hart (*Sabrina the Teenage Witch*) and Mark-Paul Gosselaar (*Saved by the Bell*) playing an alleged statutory rapist and a reluctant porn star in "Impulsive" (S9, E3; 2007) and "Sacrifice" (S3, E7; 2001), respectively. Below, we spotlight notable actors from the same show who each took a turn guest-starring on *SVU*.

JOHN STAMOS & BOB SAGET

Stamos, an actor/musician, and Saget, an accomplished stand-up/TV host, played Jesse Katsopolis and Danny Tanner (two-thirds of America's favorite co-parenting team) on *Full House*.

John Stamos: "Bang" (S12, E22; 2011)

Role: Ken Turner, a smarmy and manipulative reproductive abuser who fathered forty-seven children and pokes holes in condoms. *Have mercy!*

Bob Saget: "Choreographed" (S8, E9; 2006)

Role: Glenn Cheales, a controlling husband and engineer who covertly implants a tracking device in his wife to monitor her every move.

Did you know? While filming "Bang," Stamos met his future wife Caitlin McHugh, who played Stacy, one of his potential victims. Years later, they reconnected, fell in love, and had a son . . . on their own terms!

DEBRA MESSING & ERIC McCORMACK

Emmy-winning actors Messing and McCormick became household names as best friends Grace Adler and Will Truman on *Will & Grace*, the groundbreaking sitcom that redefined LGBTQIA+ representation on television.

Debra Messing: "Pursuit" (S12, E17; 2011)

Role: Alicia Harding, a high-profile TV journalist on a crusade against sexual predators who becomes the target of a relentless stalker.

Eric McCormack: "Sugar" (S11, E2; 2009)

Role: Vance Shepard, a cunning sugar daddy entangled in a woman's murder, who reveals a web of lies and betrayal.

Did you know? Messing's character in "Pursuit," Alicia Harding (host of the fictional TV show-within-a-show "Neighborhood Predator") was inspired by TV host Chris Hansen and his program *To Catch a Predator*. The episode gave Messing and Hargitay (close friends in real life) a chance to spend time together at work.

MILO VENTIMIGLIA & KELLY BISHOP

Ventimiglia, an Emmy-nominated actor (*This is Us*) and Bishop, a Tony-winning actress (*A Chorus Line*), played Jess Mariano and fiercely loyal matriarch Emily Gilmore on *Gilmore Girls*, respectively.

Milo Ventimiglia: "Escape" (S5, E11; 2003)

Role: Lee Healy, a man who falsely accuses his stepfather of molestation to hide his own abuse, leading to a devastating fallout when the truth is revealed.

Kelly Bishop: "Persona" (S10, E8; 2008) and **"Zebras"** (S10, E22; 2009)

Roles: Julia Zimmer, a dedicated defense attorney whose commitment to her clients ultimately leads to her tragic downfall and shocking death. Bishop had also played a registrar in "Slaves" (S1, E22; 2000).

Did you know? Bishop played Marjorie Houseman (Baby's mother) in *Dirty Dancing*, alongside *Law & Order* alum Jerry Orbach. They previously worked together in *Promises, Promises*, the 1968 musical adaptation of *The Apartment*.

MARLEE MATLIN & BRADLEY WHITFORD

Matlin was pollster Joey Lucas alongside Whitford's Emmy-winning turn as Deputy Chief of Staff Josh Lyman on *The West Wing.* Matlin became the first Deaf person to win an Oscar (*Children of a Lesser God*) and Whitford has gotten praise for *Get Out* and *The Handmaid's Tale*.

Marlee Matlin: "Painless" (S5, E22; 2004) and **"Parts"** (S6, E22; 2005)

Role: Emmy-nominated turn as Dr. Amy Solwey, a specialist dealing with chronic pain who defends assisted suicide in "Painless," and is caught up in the black-market organ trade in "Parts."

Bradley Whitford: "Reasonable Doubt" (S15, E22; 2014) and **"King of the Moon"** (S24, E15; 2023)

Role: Frank Maddox, a scheming TV producer in "Reasonable Doubt," and Pence Humphrey, a neurologist with dementia confessing to a crime he didn't commit in "King of the Moon."

Did you know? "King of the Moon" features a cheeky meta moment when Bradley Whitford's character compares Benson to Hargitay's real-life mother, Jayne Mansfield.

BRIAN BAUMGARTNER & RAINN WILSON

As fan favorites on *The Office*, Baumgartner played Kevin, the lovable accountant with a famous chili recipe, while Wilson played Dwight Schrute, assistant to the regional manager who knows the correct way to butcher a goose and is 99 percent sure he can spot the real Ben Franklin.

Brian Baumgartner: "Thought Criminal" (S15, E23; 2014)

Role: Gordon Montlieff, a pedophile caught distributing child pornography in a sting operation at his workplace.

Rainn Wilson: "Waste" (S4, E8; 2002)

Role: Mr. Baltzer, a hospital janitor questioned in a twisted case involving a comatose rape victim, unethical stem cell research, and a potential cure for Parkinson's disease.

Did You Know? Baumgartner's wardrobe in "Thought Criminal" is suspiciously similar (or a fun nod) to Dwight Schrute's iconic wardrobe, minus the glasses. But as fans of *The Office* know . . . identity theft is nothing to joke about.

FROM HOLLYWOOD TO HOMICIDE: ICONS, LEGENDS, AND OSCAR FAVORITES

In a time-honored *SVU* tradition, Hollywood's biggest stars—past and present—have traded the silver screen for the squad room, delivering some of the best guest performances on the show. From Ann Margret's Emmy-winning turn as Rita Wills in "Bedtime" (S11, E18; 2010) to Michael Shannon playing a suspected killer in "Quarry" (S6, E13; 2005), to Brooke Shields's unforgettable villainess Sheila Porter, these stars, whether they appear in just one episode or become a recurring character, are the best kind of Easter egg for fans.

ANGELA LANSBURY

With a career spanning over seven decades, Lansbury was a Broadway legend (*Gypsy, Mame, Sweeney Todd: The Demon Barber of Fleet Street*), and was beloved for her role as amateur sleuth Jessica Fletcher on *Murder, She Wrote*.

"Night" (S6, E20; 2005) and **"Day"** (*Law & Order: Trial by Jury* S1, E11; 2005)

Role: Eleanor Duvall, a manipulative matriarch who uses her power and influence to shield her son Gabriel (a serial rapist) from justice. This star-studded two-parter/crossover with *Law & Order: Trial by Jury* also features the likes of Alfred Molina, EGOT-winner Rita Moreno, and a young Bradley Cooper.

Did you know? Lansbury is fondly remembered as the voice of Mrs. Potts (alongside *Law & Order*'s Jerry Orbach as Lumiere) in Disney's *Beauty and the Beast*, the first animated film to be nominated for Best Picture at the Oscars.

WHOOPI GOLDBERG

A legendary EGOT-winning performer, Goldberg is known for *The Color Purple, Ghost* (which earned her an Oscar), and in recent years, her role as host on *The View*.

"Institutional Fail" (S17, E4; 2015)

Role: Janette Grayson, a Department of Child Services supervisor whose false welfare reports endanger lives. Her unforgettable courtroom monologue is one of the series' most powerful performances.

Did you know? This episode was inspired by the tragic real-life Gabriel Fernandez case and was praised by many social work professionals for highlighting their overwhelming and often thankless work.

ALEC BALDWIN

A Hollywood mainstay, Baldwin is known for *30 Rock*, guest appearances on *Saturday Night Live,* and film roles in *Glengarry Glen Ross*, *Beetlejuice*, and *The Departed.*

"Criminal Stories" (S15, E18; 2014)

Role: Jimmy MacArthur, a Pulitzer Prize-winning reporter for the *New York Ledger* who embeds himself with the *SVU* to profile Benson and publishes inflammatory headlines jeopardizing the case.

Did you know? Alec Baldwin, inspired by his own contentious history with the media, actually has a writing credit for the episode "Tabloid" on the original *Law & Order* in 1998.

SHARON STONE

Stone is a defining actress of the '90s known for roles in *Basic Instinct*, *The Quick and the Dead*, and *Casino* (earning her an Oscar nomination). After a near-fatal brain hemorrhage in 2001, she became a symbol of resilience and an advocate for women in Hollywood.

"Torch" (S11, E21; 2010), **"Ace"** (S11, E22; 2010), **"Wannabe"** (S11, E23; 2010), and **"Shattered"** (S11, E24; 2010)

Role: Jo Marlowe, a former NYPD officer-turned-ADA with a tragic backstory involving an aggressive cancer diagnosis and the loss of two undercover detectives.

Did you know? Stone described her experience on *SVU* as "humiliating," frustrated by the procedural format and struggling with lines after her brain aneurysm. Marlowe remains one of the show's most polarizing characters.

J.K. SIMMONS

An Oscar-winning actor for *Whiplash*, Simmons is best known as J. Jonah Jameson in Sam Raimi's *Spider-Man* trilogy and the spokesperson for Farmers Insurance.

"The Third Guy" (S1, E16; 2000), **"Wrong is Right"** (S2, E1; 2000), **"Honor"** (S2, E2; 2000), **"Legacy"** (S2, E4; 2000), **"Noncompliance"** (S2, E6; 2000), and **"Folly"** (S2, E17; 2001)

Role: Dr. Emil Skoda, an unorthodox psychiatrist assisting the SVU before Dr. Huang. Skoda was an early recurring character brought over from the original *Law & Order*.

Did you know? Dr. Emil Skoda didn't just appear in *Law & Order* properties—the first appearance of the character was actually in Dick Wolf's show *New York Undercover* in the episode "Mob Street."

VIOLA DAVIS

An acting powerhouse and EGOT winner, Viola Davis commanded the screen opposite Denzel Washington in *Fences* and earned rave reviews for her Emmy Award-winning work on *How to Get Away With Murder.*

"Mercy" (S4, E14; 2003), **"Grief"** (S4, E23; 2003), **"Birthright"** (S6, E1; 2004), **"Doubt"** (S6, E8; 2004), **"Cage"** (S8, E8; 2006), **"Cold"** (S9, E19; 2008), and **"Retro"** (S10, E5; 2008)

Role: Defense Attorney Donna Emmett, a no-nonsense lawyer with unwavering dedication to her clients, who often goes toe-to-toe with the SVU team in hard-fought courtroom battles.

Did you know? Viola Davis and Mariska Hargitay reunited in 2019 to coproduce *Emanuel*, a critically acclaimed documentary about a racially motivated mass shooting in Charleston, South Carolina that, much like *SVU*, explores themes of justice, power, and healing.

OSCAR ROYALTY

REMEMBER THESE OSCAR WINNERS ON *SVU*?

MAHERSHALA ALI – Best Supporting Actor (*Moonlight*, *Green Book*)

- "Unstable" (S11, E1; 2009)

MARY STEENBURGEN – Best Supporting Actress (*Melvin and Howard*)

- "Denial" (S3, E21; 2002)

JEREMY IRONS – Best Actor (*Reversal of Fortune*)

- "Mask" (S12, E13; 2011)
- "Totem" (S12, E20; 2011)

MARCIA GAY HARDEN – Best Supporting Actress (*Pollack*)

- "Raw" (S7, E6; 2005)
- "Informed" (S8, E1; 2006)
- "Penetration" (S12, E8; 2010)
- "Secrets Exhumed" (S14, E14; 2013)

ZOE SALDAÑA – Best Supporting Actress (*Emilia Pérez*)

- "Criminal" (S5, E21; 2004)

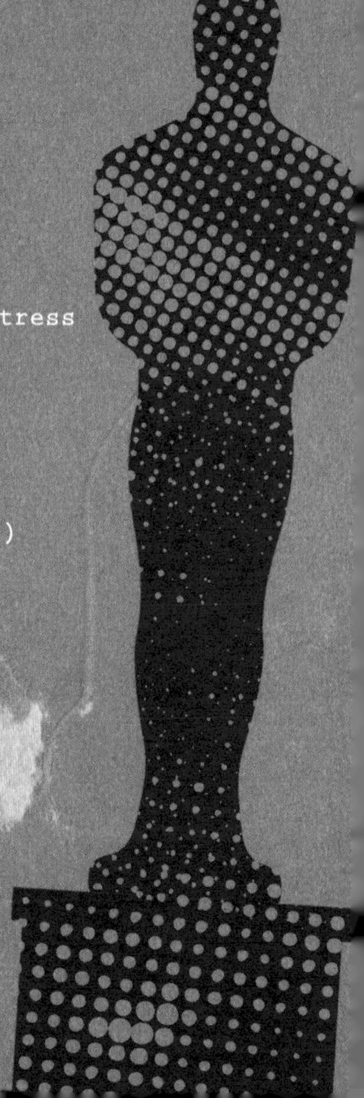

FROM STAGE TO SCREEN: BROADWAY MEETS BENSON

With *SVU* filming in the heart of New York City, it's no surprise the show is a prime destination for Broadway talent—for over two decades, listing *Law & Order* in a Playbill bio has been a rite of passage. Dick Wolf once told *The Hollywood Reporter*, "If you see an actor who doesn't have a *Law & Order* credit, it means they just got off the bus from Iowa or they really suck." During the COVID-19 pandemic, showrunner Warren Leight even made a conscious effort to hire as many Broadway actors as possible while the theater community was hit hard by an eighteen-month closure. From single guest spots to recurring roles like four-time Tony nominee Raúl Esparza (*Company*) as ADA Rafael Barba or Tony Award-winner Laura Benanti (*Gypsy*) as Maria Grazie, Broadway's best has found a second home in the *SVU* universe.

PATTI LuPONE & JEREMY JORDAN

Broadway legend Patti LuPone is a three-time Tony Award winner known for *Evita* and *Gypsy*. Jeremy Jordan is a Tony nominee known for *Newsies*, *Bonnie & Clyde*, and *The Great Gatsby*.

"Agent Provocateur" (S16, E11; 2015)

Role: LuPone plays Lydia Lebasi, a talent manager whose movie star client Skye Adderson (Jordan) becomes the focus of an investigation after a young girl is found assaulted.

Did You Know? *LMZ*, the tabloid at the center of the investigation, is a play on *TMZ*, the celebrity gossip site known for breaking entertainment news.

BILLY PORTER

A Tony and Grammy Award-winning star of *Kinky Boots* and an Emmy winner for *Pose*, Billy Porter is just one Oscar away from achieving EGOT status!

"Dissonant Voices" (S15, E7, 2013)

Role: Jackie Walker, a beloved singing coach accused of sexual abuse amid the backdrop of *American Diva*, a reality TV singing competition.

Did you know? This episode features cameos by *American Idol* contestants Taylor Hicks and Clay Aiken and recording artist Ashanti, who appear as judges on the fictional music show.

AARON TVEIT

A Tony Award-winning star of *Moulin Rouge!*, Aaron Tveit is a Broadway favorite known for *Next to Normal*, *Catch Me If You Can*, and his turn as Enjolras in the film adaptation of *Les Misérables*.

"Beef" (S11, E20; 2010) and **"Personal Fouls"** (S13, E2; 2011)

Roles: Jan Eyck, a vegetarian boyfriend of a murdered journalist in "Beef," and Stevie Harris in "Personal Fouls," a former basketball player who reveals he was molested by his coach.

Did you know? "Personal Fouls" was the debut of Detective Nick Amaro. Tveit later served on a squad himself as rookie FBI agent Mike Warren in the short-lived drama *Graceland*.

ETHAN SLATER

A Tony-nominated actor, Slater made a splash as SpongeBob in *SpongeBob SquarePants: The Broadway Musical* and later took on the role of Boq in the smash-hit feature film adaptation of Broadway's *Wicked*.

"Revenge" (S20, E4; 2018)

Role: Riley Porter, a member of an online incel community who becomes involved in a series of coordinated assaults.

Did you know? The plot was inspired by Alfred Hitchcock's film *Strangers on a Train* (1951).

EVA NOBLEZADA & ALEX BRIGHTMAN

Noblezada is a Tony-nominated actress known for her starring roles in *Hadestown* and *Miss Saigon*, while Alex Brightman earned two Tony nods for *Beetlejuice* and *School of Rock*.

"Turn Me On Take Me Private" (S22, E5; 2021)

Role: Noblezada plays Zoey Carrera, a cam girl whose client, Gabe Miller (Brightman), becomes obsessed and tracks her down in real life.

Did you know? In this episode, cult classic filmmaker John Waters plays Floyd Cougat, owner of Pornmonger and SugarFap.

AUDRA McDONALD

A six-time Tony Award-winning legend (the most all-time for any performer), McDonald is known for her powerhouse performances in *Ragtime, Porgy and Bess, Lady Day at Emerson's Bar & Grill,* and *Gypsy*.

"Contact" (S1, E19; 2000) and **"Slaves"** (S1, E22; 2000)

Role: Dr. Audrey Jackson, a forensic psychologist who helps the SVU profile a serial subway rapist and later evaluates the mental health of the squad members.

Did you know? McDonald's husband, fellow stage, film, and TV actor Will Swenson, guest-starred on *SVU* as corrupt attorney Mitch Hampton in "Broken Rhymes" (S18, E06; 2016), and also had a role in "Rock Star" (S8, E2; 2009), an episode of *Law & Order: Criminal Intent.*

MIKE FAIST

This Tony-nominated actor is known for *Dear Evan Hansen, Newsies,* and a critically acclaimed performance as Riff in Steven Spielberg's *West Side Story.*

"Complicated" (S19, E5; 2017)

Role: Glenn Lawrence, the brother of a young girl who went missing a decade earlier. When a woman claiming to be her resurfaces, it sparks a shocking investigation to uncover the truth.

Did you know? This episode features Hall of Fame basketball player Isiah Thomas. Other athletes who've appeared on *SVU* include Carmelo Anthony, Chris Bosh, and Serena Williams.

THEY'RE NOT THROWING AWAY THEIR SHOT

Several *Hamilton* original cast members have appeared on *SVU*: Tony winners Leslie Odom Jr. (playing Reverend Curtis Scott), Renée Elise Goldberry (playing Defense Attorney Martha Marron), and Daveed Diggs (playing Louis Henderson). Anthony Ramos and Okieriete Onaodowan have also made guest appearances.

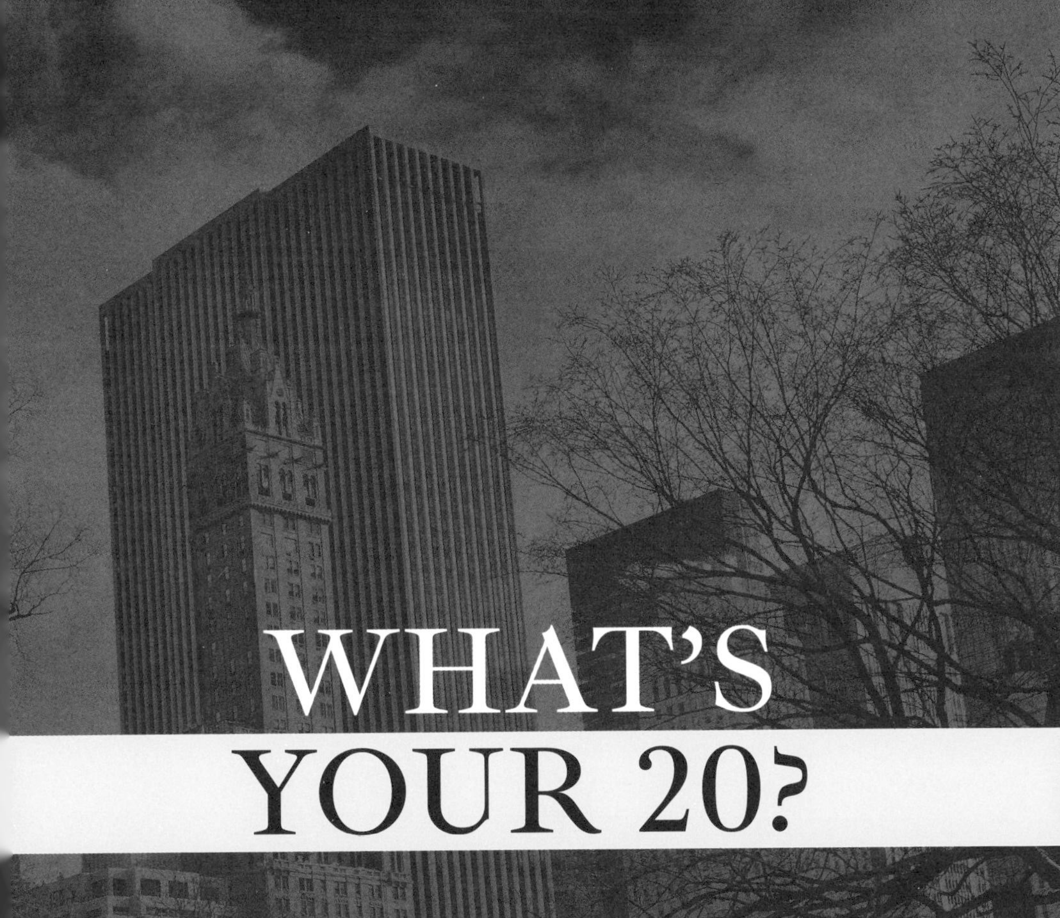

WHAT'S YOUR 20?

THE BIG APPLE

From its gritty streets and shadowed alleyways to its sleek and modern skyline, New York City's ever-evolving landscape mirrors *SVU*'s ever-changing cast of characters and their unforgettable storylines. Unlike other crime dramas, *SVU* films entirely in NYC, giving it a tangible authenticity that's nearly impossible to replicate. While most interiors are shot at film studio Chelsea Piers, the city itself provides the perfect stage for crimes, investigations, and emotional showdowns. Yet, for all the real locations shown on-screen (and there are plenty), there's also a playful wink to native New Yorkers as many of the addresses shown in the iconic transition cards (*Dun-Dun!*) are completely fictional.

So, grab this map and take a tour of both iconic real-world filming spots and legendary in-show locations. Who knows? You might even stumble upon the crew and be lucky enough to be cast as the latest VIC that Benson vows to avenge.

Yellow location symbol denotes locations that are fictional.

Red location symbol denotes real locations.

SIXTEENTH PRECINCT – FRONT/ BACK ENTRANCE & PARKING LOT

Address: 31 Chambers Street, New York, NY 10007
Latitude: N 40°42'48.6894"
Longitude: W 74°0'15.2202"

The Surrogate's Courthouse has served as the exterior for the Sixteenth Precinct and remains a key part of the show's identity. From whichever angle, the Beaux Arts-style building erected in 1907 has been the site of intense perp walks, conversations between Benson and Stabler, dramatic exits, Rollins being shot while escorting the "Dragon Lady," and the parking lot where the squad enters from on their day off to learn about William Lewis.

APARTMENT OF CAPTAIN OLIVIA BENSON

Address: 259 West 80th Street, New York, NY 10024
Latitude: N 40°47'5.5176"
Longitude: W 73°58'47.3952"

Featured in a scene in "Blood Out" (S24, E12; 2023) that left Bensler fans with more questions (and frustrations) than answers. Benson spends an eternity looking for sugar, gets within an inch of Stabler's lips—as they both clearly need some sugar of their own—before Benson turns away and the steamy moment turns to ice.

The Blueprints: In an interview, Meloni and Hargitay said that they wanted it to be a full-on kiss, but the powers that be (a.k.a. Dick Wolf) said otherwise, and he has final say.

EXTERIOR OF CAPTAIN OLIVIA BENSON APARTMENT

Address: 140 East 40th Street, New York, NY 10016
Latitude: N 40°44'58.9524"
Longitude: W 73°58'35.3928"

This Murray Hill (not Upper West Side) co-op building serves as the exterior of Benson's apartment and is shown in "Jumped In" (S24, E10; 2023) when Benson is attacked by machete-wielding members of BX9. Of course, Noah doesn't listen to instructions to stay inside and puts himself in danger. You'd think as the kid of a cop he'd learn a thing or two!

APARTMENT OF DETECTIVE OLIVIA BENSON

Address: 203 West 89th Street, New York, NY 10024
Latitude: N 40°47'23.46"
Longitude: W 73°58'25.41"

While Benson has moved house over the years, this particular address is notable for its use in the William Lewis storyline that begins during the end-of-season cliffhanger in "Her Negotiation" (S14, E24; 2013), when she's taken hostage in her own home.

The Blueprints: In real life, go three blocks south of this address to 86th Street and Amsterdam Avenue and you'll come across The Belnord Apartments, the titular building in the cozy murder mystery show *Only Murders in the Building* featuring *SVU* alum Martin Short!

APARTMENT OF DETECTIVE JOHN MUNCH

Address: 806 West 183rd Street, New York, NY 10033
Latitude: N 40°51'7.1712"
Longitude: W 73°56'16.6842"

Not shown on map.

Shown in "Uncle" (S8, E4; 2006), Munch's apartment features a full wall of books, a large print of John F. Kennedy, Jr. saluting his father's casket, and a closet adorned with a Thelonious Monk poster, a robust vinyl collection, and his firearm in a lockbox.

The Blueprints: Bennett Park, just steps away from Munch's fictional doorstep, is known as the highest natural point in Manhattan at 265 feet (81 m) above sea level.

BELLEVUE HOSPITAL CENTER

Address: 462 1st Avenue, New York, NY 10016
Latitude: N 40°44'22.5708"
Longitude: W 73°58'33.7866"

The location that housed Stabler and Munch following a courtroom shooting, took care of William Lewis after he claimed he had a seizure at Rikers, treated Stabler after he was thrown through a glass window, and accepted Mr. Kloster after he exposed his shortcomings to the courtroom. Cop-turned-shrink Dr. Rebecca Hendrix was once on staff.

The Blueprints: Established in 1736, Bellevue is the oldest public hospital in the United States, the first to offer a maternity ward and morgue in the city, the first dedicated psychiatric facility, and in 1873, the first established nursing school based on Florence Nightingale's principles.

BREAK-UP SPOT OF BENSON AND CASSIDY

Address: Meatpacking District, corner of Washington and Gansevoort Streets (facing north)
Latitude: N 40°44'21.9"
Longitude: W 74°00'28.7"

With the Standard High Line hotel in the background and the city lights glowing on their faces, Benson and Cassidy realize they have different wants and decide that, while they love each other, it's time for them to move on. If you need a spot to become "just friends" with someone, there are far worse places than this. Plus, there's an ice cream joint around the corner to cheer you up.

BROOKLYN BRIDGE

Address: New York, NY, and Brooklyn, NY
Latitude: N 40°42'32.7"
Longitude: W 74°00'02.6"

Completed in 1883, the Brooklyn Bridge is not just an NYC icon and one of the oldest bridges in the country; it's part of *SVU*'s DNA. While it's never been a show location—that honor belongs to The Mothership—it has appeared in every episode's opening credits behind "Created by Dick Wolf."

The Blueprints: For a fun challenge during the opening credits, look closely at the bridge—starting with "Monogamy" (S3, E11; 2002), there's always one light bulb burned out. Once you see it, you can't unsee it. "Monogamy" is also the first episode to use revised opening titles that edited out the Twin Towers after 9/11.

CAFÉ ANDRE

Address: 107 Hudson Street, New York, NY 10013
Latitude: N 40°43'10.4232"
Longitude: W 74°0'31.9248"

In "Loss" (S5, E4; 2003), Cabot has dinner with the entire team at this restaurant moments before she's "gunned down" in a drive-by shooting.

The Blueprints: In real life, walk around the corner at 14 North Moore Street, New York, NY 10013, and see the firehouse for Hook & Ladder Company 8, the Ghostbusters headquarters.

LAW & ORDER: SPECIAL VICTIMS UNIT
UNIVERSAL TELEVISION, LLC
STREET CLOSED FOR FILMING
THURSDAY MARCH 7TH
FRIDAY MARCH 8TH

CENTRAL PARK

Address: New York, NY
Latitude: N 40°46'27.2"
Longitude: W 73°58'15.8"

Little did Frederick Law Olmsted and Calvert Vaux know that their planned wilderness, and the world's most famous park, would be the granddaddy of locations for fictional crimes on a medium (television) that they would never enjoy during their lifetimes. Here you can track The Woodsman, talk down a grieving and suicidal father by Bow Bridge, or discover a corpse while cruising on roller blades. After all, it's a place of community and escape that sometimes harbors secrets . . .

The Blueprints: "Wet" (S12, E5; 2010) features the famous Bethesda Fountain. Atop the fountain is a statue named *Angel of the Waters*, an 1873 masterpiece by lesbian sculptor Emma Stebbins, the first woman to receive a public art commission from New York City.

CHELSEA PIERS

Address: 62 Chelsea Piers, New York, NY 10011
Latitude: N 40°44'54.2652"
Longitude: W 74°0'29.5956"

Every episode of *SVU* takes about eight days to film: four on the streets of New York City and four spent on a soundstage at *SVU*'s Silver Screen Studios at Chelsea Piers, the largest studio space in New York City. This is where all the interiors are shot for locations like the squad room, courtrooms, Benson's apartment, hospitals, and more!

The Blueprints: Chelsea Piers was originally built for passenger ships in the early 1900s, and the *Titanic* was supposed to dock at Pier 59 before its tragic end. Survivors arrived here on the *Carpathia* instead.

FORLINI'S BAR

Address: 93 Baxter Street, New York, NY 10013
Latitude: N 40°43'0.9258"
Longitude: W 73°59'58.2246"

Nestled near all the Manhattan courts, Forlini's wasn't just a cozy red-sauce Italian eatery, it was an institution for judges, ADAs, and cops in real life and on TV. Sadly, after seventy-nine years, it closed in 2022. Its final appearance was in "A Final Call at Forlini's Bar" (S23, E22; 2022).

The Blueprints: The restaurant was known for honoring patrons with plaques, including one for Edwin Torres, a former New York State Supreme Court judge and author of *Carlito's Way* (the book that the Al Pacino movie is based on) who had been a regular since 1958.

HOUSING WORKS BOOKSTORE

Address: 126 Crosby Street, New York, NY 10012
Latitude: N 40°43'28.6032"
Longitude: W 73°59'47.6874"

The interior of this bookshop was used in "Alta Kockers" (S20, E10; 2018) and in "Video Killed the Radio Star" (S23, E14; 2022) when Rollins, Carisi, and Fin go undercover at a book signing. The actual bookstore features stock that is donated, is staffed with volunteers, and gives 100 percent of its profits to fund Housing Works' lifesaving services.

The Blueprints: This bookstore was also used as a location in *All Too Well: The Short Film* written and directed by Taylor Swift.

Congratulations! You've Been Accepted to Hudson University!

"Where Prestige Meets ~~Peril~~ Productivity!"

Welcome to a top-tier academic experience with a stunning (and completely safe*) NYC campus featuring an elite law school, a world-renowned American Studies program, and the country's top safecracker, Professor Roy Batters, on staff. As for campus security . . . well, let's just say President Michelle DuBois prefers to handle things in-house.

Looking for a social life? Hudson's Greek scene is thriving—Tau Omega (and their sister chapter at Tompkins Square University) host killer parties . . . maybe just skip the punch. If you prefer secrecy, tradition, and a little harmless grooming, The Bishop Club, the oldest and most prestigious finals club, offers after-dinner brandy, sweets, and one catchy pledge song.

Extracurriculars? Dive into research, explore creative writing, visit the boathouse, party with Army cadets, stroll Alexander Hall, join a campus rally, or book a special tour with resident advisor Ken Randall. Here at Hudson, we care about our students . . . until we don't!

***Disclaimer: Once accepted to Hudson University, the school and its administration are not responsible for any murder, assault, kidnapping, or heinous crimes of any kind perpetrated by students, faculty, or administration. Accept at your own risk.**

HUDSON UNIVERSITY

Address: 504 Riverside Drive, New York, NY 10027
Latitude: N 40°48'50.7924"
Longitude: W 73°57'41.6844

More infamous than prestigious, this completely fictional university is the epicenter of heinous crimes, cover-ups, and the most despicable undergrads to ever grace a quad. Standing in for real NYC universities—to avoid tarnishing their reputation—Hudson has become such a running joke that the USA Network habitually runs a marathon called *Don't Go to Hudson University!*, full of episodes set there. *SVU* writers leaned into the gag in "Devastating Story" (S16, E18; 2015) when Benson informs baby Noah that he won't be attending that particular institution.

The Blueprints: Several locations—including office buildings, churches, and real universities like NYU, Columbia, Hunter College, Pratt Institute, CUNY, Wagner College, Barnard, and many more—stand in for Hudson's exteriors and interiors. But *SVU* isn't the only show to use Hudson. Cliff Huxtable on *The Cosby Show* earned his medical degree there (which kind of tracks), Dick Grayson (Batman's Robin), was briefly enrolled, and Jimmy Brooks on *Degrassi: The Next Generation* (played by rapper Drake) was accepted here. The mythos just keeps on growing.

MEATPACKING DISTRICT

Address: 14th Street and 9th Avenue, New York, NY 10014
Latitude: N 40°44'27.1"
Longitude: W 74°00'18.5"

A frequent source of *SVU* crime scenes, including where Benson and Stabler interrogate sex workers in "Hysteria" (S1, E4; 1999), find the dead body of a gymnast in "Pixies" (S2, E9; 2001), and where Benson goes undercover in "Beef" (S11, E20; 2010). Stroll along this trendy shopping area and the cobblestones will make you feel like you're walking with Benson and Stabler.

MERCY GENERAL HOSPITAL

Address: 365 West 32nd Street, New York, NY 10036
Latitude: N 40°44'58.887"
Longitude: W 73°59'28.14"

From Judge Donnelly being rushed in on a cliffhanger ending, to a mother waking up from amnesia and getting divorced, or the iconic first hug between Benson and Stabler, Mercy General is equipped for all types of cases. Get gold star care from Dr. Jane Larom, who helped Stabler with his temporary blindness, Benson with a temporary Zilithion poisoning, and a young woman with an RFID chip inserted . . . well, you get the idea. Dr. Celia Lee also comes highly recommended after helping Noah with his measles.

NEW YORK STATE SUPREME COURT (NEW YORK COUNTY COURTHOUSE)

Address: 60 Centre Street, New York, NY 10007
Latitude: N 40°42'51.966"
Longitude: W 74°0'7.5594"

This NYC icon, opened in 1927, is where *SVU*'s courtroom drama unfolds. Its façade bears a 1789 quotation from George Washington: "The True Administration of Justice is the Firmest Pillar of Good Government." Interiors are shot on soundstages, but its glorious steps remain one of the most recognizable show locations, often hosting some of its most tense conversations. While on *SVU* it's portrayed as a criminal courthouse, in reality this courthouse only handles civil cases—criminal trials happen down the block at 100 Centre St.

The Blueprints: This location has been used in classic films like *12 Angry Men* and perhaps the most consequential court case in all of film in *Miracle on 34th Street*, which proved that Santa Claus is real!

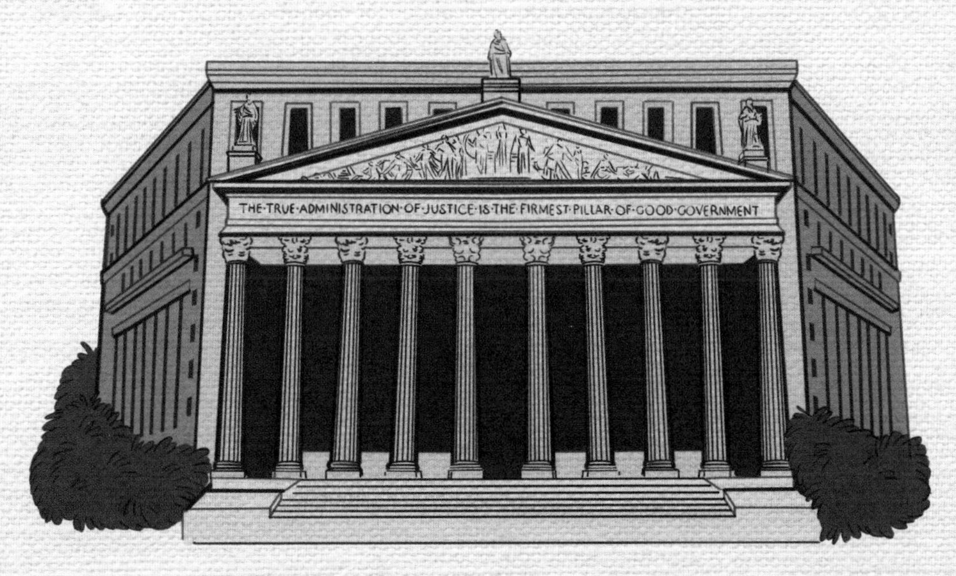

ONE POLICE PLAZA

Address: 1 Police Plaza Path, New York, NY 10038
Latitude: N 40°42'44.064"
Longitude: W 74°0'6.5118"

One Police Plaza, often abbreviated as 1PP (and sometimes referred to as "Puzzle Palace"), serves as the headquarters for the NYPD, and as Captain Cragen often laments, it is always breathing down his neck. It's home to the Computer Crimes Unit; the Internal Affairs Bureau, where Ed Tucker is frequently found scowling; and TARU, which, contrary to a common misunderstanding, is not a single person named "Taru," but rather the Technical Assistance Response Unit, offering tactical support and computer forensics.

The Blueprints: A thirty-five-foot-tall (11 m), thirty-eight-ton (34 mt) sculpture called *5 in 1* created by Tony Rosenthal is installed on the pedestrian mall of One Police Plaza. The sculpture is made of five interlocking discs that represent each of New York City's five boroughs. Installed in 1973, at the time, it was the largest metal public art sculpture in New York City.

PIER 62 SKATE PARK

Address: 143 11th Avenue, New York, NY 10011
Latitude: N 40°44'57.5802"
Longitude: W 74°0'25.326"

Located across from Chelsea Piers, this skate park was where Carisi once went undercover in "Intimidation Game" (S16, E14; 2015), which to this day is the second-lowest rated episode of the show on IMDb. Watch out for Fin hiding around the corner; he might grab you and explain what "noobz" means.

PREVITI PASTA & PIZZA

Address: 341 Lexington Avenue, New York, NY 10016
Latitude: N 40°44'58.8978"
Longitude: W 73°58'37.3404"

Grab yourself a slice like Olivia and Noah in "And a Trauma in a Pear Tree" (S24, E9; 2022). If you'd like to fully commit to the bit, ask your travel partner about your criminal father and when you'll meet Connor, your half-brother.

RIKERS ISLAND

Address: Island in the East River, Bronx, NY
Latitude: N 40°47'28.1"
Longitude: W 73°53'03.3"

New York City's infamous jail complex is a recurring presence in *SVU* (in name and reputation, if not an actual filming location) known for its harsh conditions for suspects awaiting trial or serving short sentences.

The Blueprints: Opened in 1932, Rikers Island is scheduled to close by 2027. Yet another icon that *SVU* has outlasted.

SAINT ANNE'S SHELTER

Address: 330 10th Avenue, New York, NY 10001
Latitude: N 40°45'3.9888"
Longitude: W 74°0'5.1762"

Led by nun-with-a-heart-of-gold Sister Peg, this shelter is a safe haven protecting the city's drug addicts, homeless population, and sex workers. In "Pure" (S6, E18; 2005), Sister Peg is kidnapped from the shelter and is ultimately found by Benson and Stabler in a shipping container.

SAINT MARK'S HOSPITAL

Address: 263 West 78th Street, New York, NY 10024
Latitude: N 40°47'0.2868"
Longitude: W 73°58'50.2026"

If you're a detective and your daughter overdoses on a drug and passes out, this is the hospital to take her to so she can get her stomach pumped. If you haven't caught on, we're talking about Kathleen Stabler.

SQUARE DINER

Address: 33 Leonard Street, New York, NY 10013
Latitude: N 40°43'6.6252"
Longitude: W 74°0'26.0928"

Serving the Tribeca ("Triangle Below Canal") neighborhood for over one hundred years, the Square Diner has been used as a meeting place for Benson and victims, squad members eating together, or Barba having a tense conversation with an old friend about a sexting scandal.

The Blueprints: The diner has also appeared on *Daredevil*, *Gotham*, *Crime*, *Public Morals*, and *Ray Donovan*, among other shows.

THE DAVID N. DINKINS MANHATTAN MUNICIPAL BUILDING

Address: 1 Centre Street, New York, NY 10007
Latitude: N 40°42'46.713"
Longitude: W 74°0'13.2228"

Located in Foley Square (where characters walk past *Triumph of the Human Spirit*, a sculpture by Lorenzo Pace), this location, on the show, houses the Police Crime Lab.

The Blueprints: This building is one of the largest government office buildings in the world and is named after David N. Dinkins, New York City's first African American mayor, who spent fourteen years working in the building as a city clerk.

THE NEW YORK CITY AIDS MEMORIAL

Address: 76 Greenwich Avenue, New York, NY 10011
Latitude: N 40°44'13.8618"
Longitude: W 74°0'4.3158"

The New York City AIDS Memorial was built to honor the memory of the more than one hundred thousand New Yorkers who died from AIDS. Its location in the West Village is symbolic as that was the epicenter of the epidemic and the eventual mobilization against it. It's prominently featured in "We Dream of Machine Elves" (S21, E8; 2019) when Benson drives a victim around who mentions "floating triangles" as she recalls details of an assault.

THE NEW YORK HALL OF SCIENCE

Address: 47-01 111th Street, Corona, Queens, NY 11368
Latitude: N 40°44'51.5076"
Longitude: W 73°51'6.1488"

Not shown on map.

The New York Hall of Science was featured heavily in "Lunacy" (S10, E4; 2008), which guest-starred James Brolin as Colonel Dick Finley, a marine and astronaut who was Stabler's former mentor. Its dramatic finale featured a fistfight and a rare appearance of Benson in evening wear.

The Blueprints: Located in Flushing Meadows-Corona Park, this is one of the few surviving structures from the 1964 World's Fair built alongside other landmarks like the Unisphere (the world's biggest globe) and the New York State Pavilion. While the Hall of Science was featured on *SVU*, the Unisphere and Pavilion got their own cameo in the '90s classic *Men in Black*.

THE STABLER HOUSEHOLD

Address: 72-12 Castleside Street, Glen Oaks, Queens, New York 11004
Latitude: N 40°44'43.7"
Longitude: W 73°43'29.0"

Not shown on map.

Located in a quiet, suburban area, this home serves as a sanctuary for Stabler when he tries to balance the chaos of his job with the demands of being a good (albeit overprotective) father. Whether it's sharing a tender moment with Benson on the front porch or fielding deflective answers from Maureen at 2:30 a.m., there's never a dull moment here.

WASHINGTON SQUARE PARK

Address: Washington Square, New York, NY 10012
Latitude: N 40°43'51.1566"
Longitude: W 73°59'51.3702"

One of NYC's most iconic landmarks located in the heart of Greenwich Village, and known for its towering Arch (built in 1892 to commemorate the centennial of George Washington's inauguration) as well as its lively atmosphere full of musicians, artists, and students that have made it a cultural and historical hub for decades.

The Blueprints: While filming "Silent Night, Hateful Night" (S23, E10; 2022), a singer loudly disrupted the shoot until Mariska Hargitay calmly diffused the situation. The exchange was captured on video and quickly went viral, showcasing Hargitay's kindness. Showrunner Warren Leight reposted and commented, "What other #1 on the call sheet could do this? We all ♥Mariska."

JURY DUTY

Address: 31 Saint Andrews Plaza, New York, NY 10013
Latitude: N 40°42'45.3666"
Longitude: W 74°0'11.3358"

You might recognize this spot as Wiener World (home to the best dogs in town) where Fin once taunted stalker The Weiner Man (played by Matthew Maher from *Gone Baby Gone*), in "Manipulated" (S7, E15; 2006). In real life, it's a food and drink joint called Jury Duty, a favorite of municipal workers and locals. If you visit, just make sure you don't get into trouble like The Weiner Man, unless you enjoy the feng shui of interrogation rooms.

10-4

THE JARGON OF *SVU* (A MINI-GLOSSARY)

Have you ever found yourself thinking that the detectives in *SVU* are almost speaking another language to each other? You're not alone. The show, like many other crime procedurals, throws around a lot of insider police jargon. Of course, these terms are used in real life by law enforcement professionals, but let's be honest, they also sound really cool on TV. While we couldn't cover every term uttered on the show, we've rounded up some of the most common ones that you'll hear each and every season. So, the next time a member of the squad starts rattling off terms like "10-4" (meaning "I got it") and "misdemeanor" (a lesser criminal offense punishable by fines or up to one year in jail), or flashes their "tin" (or police badge) in front of suspects, you won't have to pause and google it. Happy learning!

APB (All Points Bulletin) – This is a broadcast alert sent to law enforcement to locate a suspect or missing person. Think of it as an urgent group text—except with cops and criminals.

bracelets – Slang term for handcuffs.

bus – Slang term for an ambulance.

CI (confidential informant) – A person who provides inside information to law enforcement, often in exchange for money, a reduced sentence, or a deal.

CODIS (Combined DNA Index System) – A national DNA database helping law enforcement match samples from crime scenes with known offenders. Like 23andMe, but for criminals.

collar – Slang for an arrest. If Benson, Stabler, or any officer is precious about saying, "That's my collar," it's because they want credit for the arrest.

CompStat (comparative statistics) – A performance management system that's used to track and analyze crime trends to help cities and police departments improve their performance and reduce crime.

THE ORIGIN OF "BUS"

Primarily used in NYC and the East Coast, the slang term "bus" has various origin stories; one theory suggests it emerged in the '70s when the Grumman Corporation, which manufactured both buses and ambulances, won a contract to supply vehicles to the city. The similarity between their buses and ambulances birthed the name. Some believe the term refers to the act of picking up multiple patients during busy periods, like a bus. Yet another theory points to the derogatory use of "bus" by medics and cops stemming from the practice of patients in NYC (who don't own a car) faking medical emergencies to use ambulances as free transportation.

CSU (crime scene unit) – The forensic team called to the scene of the crime, that you see in jumpsuits or hazard gear swabbing everything for DNA or brushing for fingerprints.

DD5 – Essentially, paperwork for a particular case. A DD5 is a follow-up report documenting new case developments, from witness statements to fresh evidence. The term comes from old police slang meaning "document detectives file."

DOA (dead on arrival) – A term used for a victim who was already deceased when first responders arrived to the scene.

ESU (emergency service unit) – NYPD's elite tactical and rescue team which handles high-risk arrests, hostage situations, and emergency rescues. It's like SWAT plus search-and-rescue under one unit.

jacket – Not a piece of clothing, but a file containing records on an individual in the criminal justice system. For criminals, a jacket refers to their criminal history (similar to a rap sheet) documenting arrests, charges, and convictions. For police officers, it refers to their personnel file, including career records, commendations, and disciplinary actions. And in prison, a jacket is an inmate's case-history folder, containing institutional records.

LUDs (local usage details) – Everyone is always pulling LUDs on the show, and for good reason. They're a suspect's phone records, which are pulled to see who they called or texted before, during, or after things went sideways.

Miranda Rights – This is the famous "You have the right to remain silent" speech that every detective or officer is required to recite during an arrest. If they don't? The defense will be happy, and the *SVU*'s ADA will be very angry.

MO (modus operandi) – You probably hear something to the effect of "That's his MO" when detectives are investigating a killer. Someone's MO is a signature way of committing a crime; serial offenders tend to stick to their habits, which help detectives track them down.

perp (perpetrator) – The suspect or person believed to have committed a crime. Usually the one that gets chased down the street in dramatic foot pursuits.

THE ORIGIN OF "COLLAR" AND "COP"

The term "collar" comes from eighteenth- and nineteenth-century England, where cops would *literally* grab a suspect by the collar during an arrest. Back then, policing was a lot more hands on. Perhaps Stabler was just born in the wrong era. The term made its way to American law enforcement and stuck. And speaking of cops, the word "cop" is widely believed to have come from "copper," a reference to the metal used in early police badges. Another theory? It comes from the verb "to cop," or to seize or capture.

recant – When a witness or victim takes back their statement made to police, which on *SVU*, usually happens right before a trial and makes the detectives (and ADA) groan.

remand – Seemingly always requested by an ADA, a remand is when a judge orders a suspect to stay in custody instead of being released back in the world before trial. If a DA says "remand," the defense lawyer is about to argue "ROR."

ROR (released on recognizance) – As Persephone (Benson, undercover) taught us in "Infiltrated" (S8, E6; 2006), ROR is "released on recognizance," meaning a judge has allowed a suspect to go free without bail, trusting that they will show up in court when scheduled.

VICAP (violent criminal apprehension program) – An FBI-operated national database and analytical tool that was established in 1985 to track and analyze serial violent crimes. It helps law enforcement agencies across the US connect related crimes, track patterns, and generate leads by collecting data on unsolved homicides, sexual assaults, missing persons cases with foul play, and unidentified human remains.

EVERY SEASON THROUGH THE YEARS

THE FINAL VERDICT

You've reached the end! Well, not really—because *SVU* is like Benson's caseload: never-ending and only getting bigger. As shows come and go, as trends rise and fall, *SVU* will always remain the gold standard of crime procedurals, and its influence will forever reverberate across Hollywood and television sets around the world.

But for now, court is adjourned.

SEASON 1 (1999–2000)

Episode Count: 22
Most Viewers: "Entitled"
Highest Rating (IMDb): "Nocturne"

Season Spotlight: The Season 1 finale, "Slaves," was inspired by the notorious "Girl in the Box" case—mirroring the 1977 kidnapping of Colleen Stan. This story has been adapted in several crime procedurals including *Criminal Minds* and *Ghost Whisperer*. It's also the final episode for first showrunner Robert Palm, who departed due to the show's subject matter.

SEASON 2 (2000–2001)

Episode Count: 21
Most Viewers: "Secrets"
Highest Rating (IMDb): "Countdown"

Season Spotlight: Episode sixteen, "Runaway," had to be reshot, so Ted Kotcheff directed for twenty-four straight hours to get the new material. According to Neal Baer, it's the only episode to be broadcast only once on the network because of how poorly it turned out. Or in his words, "because it was stinky."

SEASON 3 (2001–2002)

Episode Count: 23
Most Viewers: "Monogamy"
Highest Rating (IMDb): "Ridicule"/"Denial"/"Competence"

Season Spotlight: The episode "Ridicule" broke new ground by portraying a male rape victim assaulted by women, a first for network television. One of the assailants was actress Diane Neal, before she became ADA Novak.

SEASON 4 (2002–2003)

Episode Count: 25
Most Viewers: "Dolls"
Highest Rating (IMDb): "Dominance"

Season Spotlight: Notable guest stars include John Heard & Pam Grier ("Disappearing Acts"), Titus Welliver ("Resilience"), Ari Graynor ("Damaged"), Fred Savage ("Futility"), and Joe Morton ("Grief").

SEASON 5 (2003–2004)

Episode Count: 25
Most Viewers: "Head"
Highest Rating (IMDb): "Loss"

Season Spotlight: The show was moved from its regular Friday night slot to Tuesday nights and saw an uptick in ratings. The episode "Control" marked the show's one hundredth episode, which featured a cameo by Mariska's father Mickey Hargitay.

SEASON 6 (2004–2005)

Episode Count: 23
Most Viewers: "Night"
Highest Rating (IMDb): "Conscience"

Season Spotlight: Mariska Hargitay won *SVU*'s first Golden Globe Award (Best Actress in a TV Drama, 2005). This same season also won Amanda Plummer an Emmy Award for Outstanding Guest Actress in a Drama for her episode "Weak."

SEASON 7 (2005–2006)

Episode Count: 22
Most Viewers: "Storm"
Highest Rating (IMDb): "911"

Season Spotlight: This season saw Christopher Meloni receive his first and only Emmy nomination for playing Elliot Stabler. Mariska Hargitay would win an Emmy for "911."

SEASON 8 (2006–2007)

Episode Count: 22
Most Viewers: "Scheherazade"
Highest Rating (IMDb): "Screwed"

Season Spotlight: Notable guest stars include Robert Vaughn ("Clock"), Debra Jo Rupp ("Infiltrated"), Michael K. Williams ("Underbelly"), Brian Dennehy & Paget Brewster ("Scheherazade"), Kal Penn ("Outsider"), Cary Elwes ("Dependent"), and Tim Daly ("Sin").

SEASON 9 (2007–2008)

Episode Count: 19
Most Viewers: "Signature"
Highest Rating (IMDb): "Authority" / "Undercover"

Season Spotlight: The series reached two hundred episodes with "Authority," which guest-starred Robin Williams.

SEASON 10 (2008–2009)

Episode Count: 22
Most Viewers: "Zebras"
Highest Rating (IMDb): "Zebras"

Season Spotlight: The episode "Hell," produced in collaboration with the Enough Project to truthfully portray child soldiers, was the first on-location use of the United Nations building in a TV episode.

SEASON 11 (2009–2010)

Episode Count: 24
Most Viewers: "Quickie"
Highest Rating (IMDb): "Shadow"

Season Spotlight: Oscar-winner Christine Lahti joined the cast for five episodes as ADA Sonya Paxton.

SEASON 12 (2010–2011)

Episode Count: 24
Most Viewers: "Pop"/"Possessed"
Highest Rating (IMDb): "Behave"

Season Spotlight: The first season of *SVU* not to shoot at their studio in North Bergen, New Jersey. The show relocated to Chelsea Piers, which had been occupied by The Mothership.

SEASON 13 (2011–2012)

Episode Count: 23
Most Viewers: "Lost Traveller"
Highest Rating (IMDb): "Spiraling Down"

Season Spotlight: The season premiere "Scorched Earth" was a dramatization of the scandal around IMF (International Monetary Fund) chief Dominique Strauss-Kahn, and "Blood Brothers" was inspired by the Arnold Schwarzenegger scandal.

SEASON 14 (2012–2013)

Episode Count: 24
Most Viewers: "Beautiful Frame"
Highest Rating (IMDb): "Dreams Deferred"

Season Spotlight: Production was shut down briefly during Hurricane Sandy. The show's Chelsea Piers studio lost power and had water damage. Nevertheless, the show celebrated "Manhattan Vigil" as its landmark three hundredth episode.

SEASON 15 (2013–2014)

Episode Count: 24
Most Viewers: "Surrender Benson"/"Imprisoned Lives"
Highest Rating (IMDb): "Surrender Benson"

Season Spotlight: "American Tragedy" fictionalized the 2012 Trayvon Martin shooting as well as incorporated story beats from the Paula Deen racism scandal, with Cybill Shepherd guest starring as a Deen-like celebrity Southern chef.

SEASON 16 (2014–2015)

Episode Count: 23
Most Viewers: "Girls Disappeared"
Highest Rating (IMDb): "Daydream Believer"

Season Spotlight: In "Glasgowman's Wrath," *SVU* took inspiration from the infamous Slender Man stabbing case in Waukesha, WI (where two twelve-year-olds stabbed a classmate to please "Slender Man") and released it shortly after the real crime occurred, making it a true ripped-from-the-headlines episode.

SEASON 17 (2015–2016)

Episode Count: 23
Most Viewers: "Devil's Dissections"/"Criminal Pathology"
Highest Rating (IMDb): "Heartfelt Passages"

Season Spotlight: Rollins's pregnancy storyline paralleled star Kelli Giddish giving birth to her first child in October 2015.

SEASON 18 (2016–2017)

Episode Count: 21
Most Viewers: "Terrorized"
Highest Rating (IMDb): "Motherly Love"

Season Spotlight: The 400th episode was initially billed as the Mariska Hargitay-directed "Motherly Love," but due to episode reshuffling, that episode aired as the 399th. "Great Expectations" became the official 400th episode and aired on February 15th, 2017.

SEASON 19 (2017–2018)

Episode Count: 24
Most Viewers: "Something Happened"
Highest Rating (IMDb): "Gone Baby Gone"

Season Spotlight: Inspirations for episodes included the Harvey Weinstein scandal ("Flight Risk") and the Gypsy Rose Blanchard case ("Pathological").

SEASON 20 (2018–2019)

Episode Count: 24
Most Viewers: "Man Up"/"Man Down"
Highest Rating (IMDb): "Alta Kockers"

Season Spotlight: Actress Lucy Liu directed the episode "Dearly Beloved."

SEASON 21 (2019–2020)

Episode Count: 20
Most Viewers: "Solving for the Unknowns"
Highest Rating (IMDb): "Murdered at a Bad Address"

Season Spotlight: This season *SVU* made history, officially becoming the longest-running US live-action primetime series. On the season's premiere day, Dick Wolf and Mariska Hargitay rang the opening bell at the New York Stock Exchange as a nod to the show's cultural impact.

SEASON 22 (2020–2021)

Episode Count: 16
Most Viewers: "Return of the Prodigal Son"
Highest Rating (IMDb): "Post-Graduate Psychopath"

Season Spotlight: The long-awaited reunion of Benson and Stabler took place on April 1st, 2021, as part of a crossover that launched Stabler's spin-off, *Law & Order: Organized Crime*. Their reunion drew over eight million live viewers and trended #1 worldwide on Twitter.

SEASON 23 (2021–2022)

Episode Count: 22
Most Viewers: "And the Empire Strikes Back"/"Never Turn Your Back on Them"
Highest Rating (IMDb): "The Five Hundredth Episode"

Season Spotlight: The season's sixth episode, fittingly titled "The Five Hundredth Episode," was the latest milestone for the show. Detective Nick Amaro and Captain Donald Cragen returned to help the squad with the case.

SEASON 24 (2022–2023)

Episode Count: 22
Most Viewers: "Blood Out"
Highest Rating (IMDb): "King of the Moon"

Season Spotlight: The episode "King of the Moon" was dedicated to the memory of Richard Belzer, who had passed away a few days before the episode was released. Mariska Hargitay directed the episode and later wrote on Instagram, "Goodbye my dear, dear friend. I will miss you, your unique light, and your singular take on this strange world."

SEASON 25 (2024)

Episode Count: 13
Most Viewers: "Tunnel Blind"
Highest Rating (IMDb): "Marauder"

Season Spotlight: This season was delayed and shortened due to the 2023 Writers Guild and SAG-AFTRA strikes, which marked the first time that *SVU* missed its fall premiere since 1999. The show explained the time jump by having Benson return from a months-long FBI training program.

SEASON 26 (2024–2025)

Episode Count: 22
Most Viewers: "Master Key"
Highest Rating (IMDb): "Cornered"

Season Spotlight: This season saw several departures on both sides of the screen: Fan favorite Octavio Pisano (Det. Joe Velasco) left after four seasons; newcomer Juliana Aidén Martinez (Det. Kate Silva) exited after one season to make room for the return of Kelli Giddish as Detective Kim Rollins; and David Graziano stepped down as showrunner—paving the way for longtime *SVU* writer Michele Fazekas, who will become the first woman showrunner in the program's history.

ACKNOWLEDGMENTS

The investigation comes to a close . . .

Every good detective knows you can't solve a case alone—you need a top-notch squad, a few solid leads, and the patience to comb through hours and hours of evidence. Or, in this case, hundreds of *SVU* episodes.

First, to my wife—thank you for enduring countless heinous acts on TV before bedtime and never objecting to "just one more episode." What started as research quickly turned into a dinner-time binge ritual. To my family and friends, as always, thanks for your support and understanding while my schedule revolved around this book. To anyone who commented or voted on my social media posts, thanks for your insight. And to The Brown Cow Ice Cream Parlor—your brownie sundae kept me from going full Stabler during hard writing days.

Special thanks to Vicki Whooper, for your expert *SVU* guidance, and to Bethany Speer, for being a great confidential informant. To the SVU Fandom Wiki Page—your exhaustive research was invaluable. I hope you don't mind, but after binging this show, I had to correct a few things. Consider it my own small contribution to seeking justice. And to the detectives over at r/SVU—your love for this show is unmatched. I'm honored to be in the same precinct.

To the talented cast and crew of Riverside-Brookfield High School's smash-hit production of *Rock of Ages*—getting to work with you all while writing this book kept me energized and inspired.

To my own Special Authors Unit, I couldn't have finished this investigation without your assistance. Thanks to my agent, Justin Brouckaert of Aevitas Creative Management—like Captain Cragen, you assigned me this case and watched over me with expert dad energy. To my wonderful editor, Flannery Wiest—like Melinda

Warner, Ryan O'Halloran, and TARU's Ruben Morales, you took all the evidence I collected, analyzed it, deciphered it, and presented it back to me with expert precision and care. For that, you deserve a commendation. And to the rest of the Quarto team, including Nicole James, the uber-talented design team, and anyone else whose talents touched this book—I'm forever grateful that you made my case strong enough for any ADA to win in court.

Case closed. But as any good detective—or amateur sleuth—knows, there's always another mystery around the corner . . .

DUN-DUN.

ABOUT THE AUTHOR

Neal E. Fischer is an award-winning filmmaker, author, podcaster, and pop culture fanatic. When he's not directing films, commercials, theater, and social media content, he's cohosting the podcasts *Triviality* and *Curated by Chance,* appearing on game shows like *The Floor*, or writing fun books like this one! His past subjects include Patrick Swayze, iconic TV shows and their sets, Christmas movie and rom-com trivia, and totally awesome biographies for kids about Steph Curry, Cristiano Ronaldo, and MrBeast.

A former band geek, theater nerd, prom king, and unapologetic boy band fan, Neal was raised on movies totally inappropriate for a five-year-old—but clearly, he turned out just fine. In any rare moments of free time, he loves traveling the world to film/TV locations, seeing Broadway shows, and visiting cute coffee shops alongside his wife, Colleen, a theater director and special education instructor. They live in Chicago.

Find Neal on social media @nealefischer or at www.nealefischer.com.

For Papa and Grandma—because if there's a Dick Wolf show out there, you've probably seen every episode . . . twice. Thanks for the inspiration. And for Fafa—thank you for your endless curiosity and for being a bright light in an often grey world. I'll miss you.

First published in 2025 by Epic Ink, an imprint of The Quarto Group, 142 West 36th Street, 4th Floor, New York, NY 10018, USA
(212) 779-4972
www.Quarto.com

EEA Representation, WTS Tax d.o.o., Žanova ulica 3, 4000 Kranj, Slovenia.
www.wts-tax.si

Epic Ink titles are also available at discount for retail, wholesale, promotional, and bulk purchase. For details, contact the Special Sales Manager by email at specialsales@quarto.com or by mail at The Quarto Group, Attn: Special Sales Manager, 100 Cummings Center Suite 265D, Beverly, MA 01915 USA.

10 9 8 7 6 5 4 3 2 1

ISBN: 978-0-7603-9854-8

Digital edition published in 2025
eISBN: 978-0-7603-9855-5

Library of Congress Control Number: 2025936077

Group Publisher: Rage Kindelsperger
Creative Director: Laura Drew
Managing Editor: Cara Donaldson
Acquisition Editor: Nicole James
Editor: Flannery Wiest
Text: Neal E. Fischer
Art Director: Scott Richardson
Cover Design: Scott Richardson
Interior Design: Maeve Bargman
Illustrator: Simone Douglas

Printed in Huizhou, Guangdong, China
TT072025